APR 1 0 2002

india

Editing: Dr. Vasant Joshi, PhD, Kamaal, Sarito, Yoga Pratap Bharati
Design: Amiyo, Harito
Production: Harito
Photography©:   Raghu Rai, title page
                Raghu Rai, pp. 5, 112, 164 & 165
                www.dinodia.com, jacket backside, pp. 24, 63, 177, 183
                Indra Sabha/www.dinodia.com, p. 23
                Haridvar/www.dinodia.com, pp. 52 & 53
                Carlos Navajas/Image Bank International, 2001, p. 101
                Harald Sund/Image Bank International, 2001, p. 109
                Osho International Foundation, remaining photos
Color separation: Unique Photo Offset Services, Mumbai
Printed in China

All text has been excerpted from published, extemporaneous works by Osho.

Osho is a registered trademark of Osho International Foundation, used under license. www.osho.com

ISBN 0-312-28824-7

First published in India as: *India My Love — Fragments of a Golden Past* by The Rebel Publishing House Pvt. Ltd.

First U.S. Edition: January 2002

10 9 8 7 6 5 4 3 2 1

OSHO

india
my love

a spiritual journey

ST. MARTIN'S PRESS   NEW YORK

OSHO

india
my love

CONTENTS

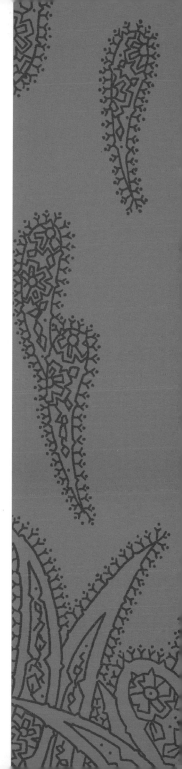

introduction

INDIA IS NOT JUST

GEOGRAPHY OR

HISTORY....

IT IS VIBRATING

WITH CERTAIN

ENERGY FIELDS WHICH

NO OTHER COUNTRY

CAN CLAIM.

INTRODUCTION

India is not just geography or history. It is not only a nation, a country, a mere piece of land. It is something more: it is a metaphor, poetry, something invisible but very tangible. It is vibrating with certain energy fields which no other country can claim.

For almost ten thousand years, thousands of people have reached to the ultimate explosion of consciousness. Their vibration is still alive, their impact is in the very air; you just need a certain perceptivity, a certain capacity to receive the invisible that surrounds this strange land.

It is strange, because it has renounced everything for a single search, the search for the truth. It has not produced great philosophers — you will be surprised to know it — no Plato, no Aristotle, no Thomas Aquinas, no Kant, no Hegel, no Bradley, no Bertrand Russell. The whole history of India has not produced a single philosopher — and they have been searching for truth!

Certainly their search was very different from the search that has been done in other countries.

In other countries people were thinking about truth; in India, people were not thinking about truth — because how can you think about truth? Either you know it, or you don't; thinking is impossible, philosophy is impossible. It is absolutely an absurd and futile exercise. It is just like a blind man thinking about light — what can he think? He may be a great genius, may be a great logician — it is not going to help. Neither logic is needed nor genius is needed; what is needed is eyes to see.

Light can be seen, but cannot be thought. Truth can be seen, but cannot be thought; hence we don't have a parallel word in India for "philosophy." The search for truth we call *darshan*, and *darshan* means seeing.

"Philosophy" means thinking, and thinking is circular — about and about, it never reaches to the point of experiencing.

India is the only land in the whole world, strangely, which has devoted all its talents in a concentrated effort to see the truth and to be the truth.

You cannot find a great scientist in the whole history of India. It is not that there were not talented people, it is not that there were not geniuses. Mathematics was founded in India, but it did not produce Albert Einstein. The whole country, in a miraculous way, was not interested in any objective research. To know the other has not been the goal here, but to know oneself.

For ten thousand years millions of people persistently making a single effort, sacrificing everything for it — science, technological development, riches — accepting poverty, sickness, disease, death, but not dropping the search at any cost...it has created a certain noosphere, a certain ocean of vibrations around you.

If you come here with a little bit of a meditative mind, you will come in contact with it. If you come here just as a tourist, you will miss it. You will see the ruins, the palaces, the Taj Mahal, the temples, Khajuraho, the Himalayas, but you will not see India — you will have passed through India without meeting it. It was everywhere, but you were not sensitive, you were not receptive. You will have come here to see something which is not truly India but only its skeleton — not its soul. And you will have photographs of its skeleton and you will make albums of its skeleton, and you will think that you have been to India and you know India, and you are simply deceiving yourself.

There is a spiritual part. Your cameras cannot photograph it; your training, your education cannot capture it.

You can go to any country, and you are perfectly capable of meeting the people, the country, its history, its past — in Germany, in Italy, in France, in England. But you cannot do the same as far as India is concerned. If you try to categorize it with other countries, you have already missed the point, because those countries don't have that spiritual aura. They have not produced a Gautam Buddha, a Mahavira, a Neminatha, an Adinatha...they have not produced a Kabir, a Farid, a Dadu. They have produced scientists, they have produced poets, they have produced great artists, they have produced painters, they have produced all kinds of talented people. But the mystic is India's monopoly; at least up to now it has been so.

And the mystic is a totally different kind of human being. He's not simply a genius, he's not simply a great painter or a great poet — he is a vehicle of the divine, a provocation, an invitation for the divine. He opens the doors for the divine to come in. And for thousands of years, millions of people have opened the doors for the divine to fill the atmosphere of this country. To me, that atmosphere is the real India. But to know it, you will have to be in a certain state of mind.

When you are meditating, trying to be silent, you are allowing the real India to come in contact with you. You can find truth in this poor country in a way you cannot find anywhere else. It is utterly poor, and yet spiritually it has such a rich heritage that if you can open your eyes and see that heritage you will be surprised. Perhaps this is the only country which has been deeply concerned with the evolution of consciousness and nothing else. Every other country has been concerned with a thousand other things. But this country has been one-pointed, a single goal: how human consciousness can be evolved to a point where it meets with the divine; how to bring the human and the divine closer.

And it is not a question of one person, but millions of people; not a question of a day or a month or a year, but thousands of years. Naturally, it has created a tremendous energy field around the country. It is all over the place, you just have to be ready.

It is not coincidental that whenever anybody is thirsty for truth, suddenly he has become interested in India, suddenly he has started moving towards the East. And it is not only today, it is as old as there are records. Pythagoras, twenty-five centuries ago, came to India in search of truth. Jesus Christ came to India....

...And down the centuries, seekers have been coming to this land from all over the world. The country is poor, the country has nothing to offer, but to those who are sensitive, it is the richest place on the earth. But the richness is of the inner. This poor country can give you the greatest treasure that is possible for human beings.

the universal dream

THE DREAM

OF THE BUDDHAS

HAS ALWAYS BEEN

TO REMIND YOU

OF THAT WHICH

HAS BEEN

FORGOTTEN,

TO AWAKEN

THAT WHICH IS

ASLEEP IN YOU.

The dream is universal, it is not my own. It is centuries old — or you can say, it is eternal. The earth began to see that dream with the dawning of the very first rays of human consciousness. How many flowers are strung in the garland of this dream — how many Gautam Buddhas, Mahaviras, Kabirs and Nanaks have sacrificed their lives for this dream? How am I to call that dream mine? That dream is the dream of man himself, of man's own inner self. We have given this dream a name — we call this dream India.

India is not a piece of land or some political entity or a part of some historical facts. It is not a mad race for money, power, position and prestige. India is a longing, a thirst to attain truth — the truth that resides in every heartbeat of ours, the truth that is lying asleep under the layer of our consciousness, the truth that is ours but yet forgotten. Its remembrance, its reclamation, is India.

"*Amritasya putrah,*" Oh, sons of the immortal! — only those who have heard this call are truly citizens of India. Nobody else becomes a citizen of India. You can be born anywhere on the earth — in any country, in any century; in the past or in the future: if your search is the search for the inner, you are a son of India. For me, India and spirituality are synonymous. India and religiousness are synonymous. In this sense, the sons of India are in each nook and corner of this earth. And those who have been born in India accidentally, as long as they have not felt a passion in the search for the deathless, they have no right to be called citizens of India.

India is an eternal journey, a path of nectar, stretching from eternity to eternity. This is why we have never written any history of India. Is history something worth writing? History is the name for the ordinary, the mundane everyday happenings which rise like a storm today but tomorrow not even a trace of them is left. History is just a whirlwind of dust.

India has never written history, India has only tried to touch the eternal, in the same manner as a *chakor,* a red-legged partridge, goes on gazing at the moon, without even blinking....

I want to remind those who have forgotten, awaken those who have fallen asleep, so that India can regain its inner dignity, its pride, its snow-capped peaks — because the destiny of the whole of humanity is linked with the destiny of India. It is not only a matter of one country: if India is lost in darkness, man has no future. And if we are able to give India its wings again, its sky again, fill its eyes again with a longing to fly towards the stars, we will not only save those who have an inner thirst, we will also save the ones who are asleep today, but who will become awakened tomorrow.

The destiny of India is the destiny of the whole of humanity — because of the way we have refined human consciousness, because of the lamps we have lit within man, because of the flowers that we have cultivated in man, the fragrance we have created in man. Nowhere else in the world has this been done. It has been ten thousand years of ceaseless perseverance, of ceaseless yoga, of ceaseless meditation. And for the sake of this, we have lost everything else. For the sake of this we have sacrificed everything else. But even in the darkest nights of man we have kept the lamp of man's consciousness lit. No matter how dim the flame may have become, that lamp still burns....

You ask me, what is my dream? It is the same as the dream of the buddhas has always been: to remind you of that which has been forgotten, to awaken that which is asleep in you. Because until man understands that eternal life is his very birthright, that godliness is his birthright, he will not be able to become whole; he will remain incomplete, crippled.

Since I have become awakened, each moment, every hour, there is only one effort, only one endeavor, day and night only one attempt — that somehow I may be able to remind you of your forgotten treasure; that the declaration, *"Ana'l haq"* can also arise from within you, that you can also say, *"Aham Brahmasmi,"* I am God.

God has been talked about in every corner of the world, but God has always remained far away, beyond the stars. Only India has established that God is within man. And in realizing the God within man, only India has given man the capability, the dignity and the beauty of he himself becoming the temple, the shrine.

How every being can become a temple, and how each being, in each moment, can become a prayer — this you can call my dream. [1]

"*Aham Brahmasmi*" is perhaps the boldest statement ever made by any human being in any age in any part of the world, and I don't think it can be improved upon in the future, ever. Its courage is so absolute and perfect that you cannot refine it, you cannot polish it. It is so fundamental that you cannot go deeper than this, neither can you go higher than this. This simple statement, "*Aham Brahmasmi*," in Sanskrit, is only three words. In English also it can be translated in these few words: "I am the Ultimate." Beyond me there is nothing; there is no height that is not within me and there is no depth which is not within me. If I can explore myself I have explored the whole mystery of existence.

The days of the Upanishads in this land were the most glorious. The only search, the only seeking, the only longing, was to know oneself — no other ambition ruled mankind. Riches, success, power, everything was absolutely mundane. Those who were ambitious, those who were running after riches, those who wanted to be powerful were considered to be psychologically sick. And those who were really healthy psychologically, spiritually healthy, their only search was to know oneself and to be oneself and to declare to the whole universe the innermost secret. That secret is contained in this statement, "*Aham Brahmasmi*." [2]

...The teachings of the Upanishads are much older than Buddha. What Buddha has said is the same as what lies hidden in the Upanishads. Those who penetrate deeply into it will find that Buddha has given a living commentary on the Upanishads....

The sages of the Upanishads were playing with fire, but by the time Buddha arrived on the scene, it had already turned to ashes. When Buddha again began to talk about fire, it was only natural that to those who were guarding the ashes and calling it fire, he appeared as their enemy. This is natural, because if the fire is lit again, the guardians of the ashes will fall in a great difficulty....

It is difficult to understand that truth is always one. Only its expressions are new; the life-core of truth is always the same....

In fact, whatsoever is of eternal value has been so well told in the Upanishads that sometimes I wonder if it is at all possible to add anything to them which is not already there. Can the Upanishads be refined any further? Can they be improved upon? — I doubt it. It seems to be very difficult to make any improvement. It is doubtful that it can be done; there seems to be no way. [3]

It happened in Upanishadic days that one young boy, Svetaketu, was sent by his father to a *guru-kul*, to a family of an enlightened master, to learn. He learned everything that could be learned, he memorized all the Vedas and all the science available in those days. He became proficient in them, he became a great scholar; his fame started spreading all over the country. Then there was nothing else to be taught, so the master said, "You have known all that can be taught. Now you can go back." ❧ Thinking that everything had happened and there was nothing else — because whatsoever the master knew, he also knew, and the master had taught him everything — Svetaketu went back. Of course with great pride and ego, he came back to his father. ❧ When he was entering the village his father, Uddalak, looked out of the window at his son coming back from the university. He saw the way he was walking very proudly, the way he was holding his head in a very egoistic way, the way he was looking around, very self-conscious that he knew. The father became sad and depressed, because this is not the way of someone who really knows, this is not the way of one who has come to know the supreme knowledge. ❧ The son entered the house. He was thinking that his father would be very happy — he had become one of the suprememost scholars of the country, he was known everywhere, respected everywhere — but he saw that the father was sad, so he asked, "Why are you sad?" ❧ The father said, "Only one question I have to ask you. Have you learned that by learning which there is no need to learn anything more? Have you known that by knowing which all suffering ceases? Have you been taught that which cannot be taught?"  The boy also became sad. He said, "No. Whatsoever I know has been taught to me, and I can teach it to anybody who is ready to learn." The father said, "Then you go back and ask your master that you be taught that which cannot be taught." The boy said, "But that is absurd. If it cannot be taught, how can the master teach me?" The father said, "That is the art of the master: he can teach you that which cannot be taught. You go back." He went back. Bowing down to his master's feet, he said, "My father has sent me for an absolutely absurd thing. Now I don't know where I am and what I am asking you. My father has told me to come back and return only when I have learned that which cannot be learned, when I have been taught that which cannot be taught. What is it? What is this? You never told me about it." The master said, "Unless one inquires, it cannot be told; you never inquired about it. But now you are starting a totally different journey. And remember, it cannot be taught so it is very

delicate; only indirectly can I help you. Do one thing: take all the animals of my *gurukul*"— there were at least four hundred cows, bulls and other animals — "and go to the deepest forest possible where nobody ever comes and moves. Live with these animals in silence. Don't talk, because these animals cannot understand any language. So remain silent, and when just by reproduction these four hundred animals have become one thousand, then come back." It was going to be a long time — until four hundred animals had become one thousand. And he was to go without saying anything, without arguing, without asking, "What are you telling me to do? Where will it lead?" He was just to live with animals and trees and rocks; not talking, and forgetting the human world completely. Because your mind is a human creation, if you live with human beings the mind is continuously fed. They say something, you say something — the mind goes on learning, it goes on revolving. "So go," the master said, "to the hills, to the forest. Live alone. Don't talk. And there is no use in thinking, because these animals won't understand even

your thinking. Drop all your scholarship here."
◈ Svetaketu followed. He went to the forest and lived with the animals for many years. For a few days thoughts remained there in the mind — the same thoughts repeating themselves again and again. Then it became boring. If no new thoughts are felt, then you will become aware that the mind is just repetitive, just a mechanical repetition; it goes on in a rut. And there was no way to get new knowledge. With new knowledge the mind is always happy, because there is something again to grind, something again to work out; the mechanism goes on moving. ◈ Svetaketu became aware. There were four hundred animals, birds, other wild animals, trees, rocks, rivers and streams, but no man and no possibility of any human communication. There was no use in being very egoistic, because these animals didn't know what type of great scholar this Svetaketu was. They didn't consider him at all; they didn't look at him with respect, so by and by the pride disappeared, because it was futile and it even looked foolish to walk in a prideful way with the animals. Even Svetaketu started feeling, "If I remain egoistic these animals will laugh at

me — so what am I doing?" Sitting under the trees, sleeping near the streams, by and by his mind became silent. ◈ The story is beautiful. The years passed and his mind became so silent that Svetaketu completely forgot when he had to return. He became so silent that even this idea was not there. The past dropped completely, and with the dropping of the past the future drops, because the future is nothing but a projection of the past — just the past reaching into the future. So he forgot what the master had said, he forgot when he had to return. There was no when and where, he was just here and now. He lived in the moment just like the animals; he became a cow. ◈ The story says that when the animals became one thousand, they started feeling uncomfortable. They were waiting for Svetaketu to take them back to the ashram and he had forgotten, so one day the cows decided to speak to Svetaketu and they said, "Now it is time enough, and we remember that the master had said that you must come back when the animals became one thousand, and you have completely forgotten. Now is the time and we must go back. We have become one thousand." ◈ So Svetaketu went back with the animals. The master looked from the door of his hut at Svetaketu coming with one thousand animals, and he said to his other disciples, "Look, one thousand and one animals are coming." Svetaketu had become such a silent being — no ego, no self-consciousness, just moving with the animals as one of them.  The master came to receive him; the master was dancing, ecstatic. He embraced Svetaketu and he said, "Now there is nothing to say to you — you have already known. Why have you come? There is no need to come now, there is nothing to be taught. You have already known."  Svetaketu said, "Just to pay my respects, just to touch your feet, just to be grateful. It has happened, and you have taught me that which cannot be taught." [4]

The word "mysticism" comes from a Greek word, *mysterion*, which means "secret ceremony." The people who have touched the unknowable gather together to share. The sharing is not verbal; it cannot be verbal. The sharing is of their being; they pour their being into each other. They dance together, they sing together, they look into each other's eyes, or they simply sit silently together. That's what was being done with Buddha, with Krishna, with Jesus, in different ways.

The lovers of Krishna were dancing with him. That was a *mysterion*, a secret ceremony. If you look from the outside at what is happening you will not be able to know what is really the case. Unless you become a participant, unless you dance with Krishna, you will not know what is being shared, because that which is being shared is invisible. It is not a commodity, it cannot be transferred from one hand to another; you will not see anything happening like that. It is not objective. It is the flowing of one being into another, flowing of the presence of the master into the disciple.

These kinds of secret ceremonies in India have been called *ras*; in the tradition of Krishna they are called "ras." *Ras* means dancing with the master, so that your energy is flowing and the master's energy is flowing. And only flowing energies can have a meeting. Stagnant pools cannot meet, only rivers can meet. It is only through movement that meeting is possible.

But the same was happening with Buddha too, with no visible dance. Buddha was sitting silently, his disciples were sitting silently; it was called *satsang*, "being with truth." Buddha has become enlightened, he is a light unto himself. Others who are not yet lit, whose candles are yet unlit, sit in close proximity, in intimacy, in deep love and gratitude, come closer and closer to Buddha in their silence, in their love. Slowly, slowly a moment comes, the space between the master and the disciple disappears — and the jump of the flame from the master to the disciple. The disciple is ready to receive it; the disciple is nothing but a welcome. The disciple is feminine, a receptivity, a womb. This too is a *mysterion*, a secret ceremony. [5]

The lotus flower has been very symbolic to the East, because the East says you should live in the world but remain untouched by it. You should remain in the world, but the world should not remain in you. You should pass through the world without carrying any impression, any impact, any scratch. If by the time of death you can say that your consciousness is as pure, as innocent as you have brought with you at birth, you have lived a religious life, a spiritual life.

Hence the lotus flower has become a symbol of a spiritual style of living. Untouched by the water...it grows from the mud in the water, and yet remains untouched. And it is a symbol of transformation. Mud is transformed into the most beautiful and the most fragrant flower this planet knows about. Gautam Buddha was so much in love with the lotus that he called his paradise "the Lotus Paradise." [6]

One morning a great king, Prasenjita, came to Gautam Buddha. In one of his hands he had a beautiful lotus flower and in the other hand one of the most precious diamonds of those days. He had come because his wife was persistent: "When Gautam Buddha is here, you waste your time with idiots, talking about unnecessary things." ॐ From her very childhood she had been going to Gautam Buddha; then she got married. Prasenjita had no inclination of that kind, but because she was so insistent he said, "It is worth at least one visit to go and see what kind of man this is." But he was a man of very great ego, so he took out the most precious diamond from his treasure to present to Gautam Buddha. ॐ He did not want to go there just as an ordinary man. Everybody had to know.... In fact he wanted everybody to know, "Who is greater — Gautam Buddha or Prasenjita?" That diamond was so precious that many fights had happened, wars had happened over it. ॐ His wife laughed and she said, "You are absolutely unaware of the man I'm taking you to. It is better that you take a flower rather than a stone to present to him." He could not understand, but he said, "There is no harm. I can take both. Let us see." ॐ When he reached there, he offered his diamond, which he was carrying in one of his hands, and Buddha said simply, "Drop it!" Naturally, what can you do? – he dropped it. He thought that perhaps his wife was right. In the other hand he was carrying the lotus, and as he tried to offer the lotus, Buddha said, "Drop it!" ॐ He dropped that too, and became a little

20

afraid: the man seems to be insane, but ten thousand disciples.... And he stood there thinking that the people must be thinking he is stupid. And Buddha said the third time, "Don't you listen to me? Drop it!" Prasenjita said, "He is really gone. Now I have dropped the diamond, I have dropped the lotus; now I don't have anything." And at that very moment, Sariputta, an old disciple of Gautam Buddha, started laughing. His laughter made Prasenjita turn towards him, and he asked him, "Why are you laughing?" He said, "You don't understand the language. He is not saying drop the diamond, he is not saying drop the lotus. He is saying drop yourself, drop the ego. You can have the diamond and you can have the lotus, but drop the ego. Don't take it back with you." Those were beautiful days. Suddenly a new sky opened to Prasenjita. He dropped himself at Gautam Buddha's feet in utter humbleness, and he never left. He became part of the great caravan that used to follow Gautam Buddha. He forgot all about his kingdom, forgot about everything. The only thing that remained was this beautiful man, this tremendous grace, this invisible magnetism, these eyes and this silence. And he was gripped by all this. It is not a question of belief. It is not a question of conversion, argumentation — it is a question of the highest quality of love. 7

Meditation never died in this country. Sometimes above ground, sometimes underground, but its river has remained flowing constantly, eternally. It flows today, it will flow tomorrow also — and that is the only hope for man. Because the day meditation dies, man will also die. Man's actuality is meditation. You may be aware of it or you may not be, you may know it or you may not, but meditation is your inner core. That which is hidden within your breath, that which is hidden within your heartbeats, that which you are, is nothing other than meditation.

...If this country has given the world anything, if there is any contribution, it is only meditation. Then whether in the form of Patanjali or in the form of Mahavira or in the form of Buddha or in the form of Kabir or in the form of Nanak — names may have been changing but the contribution has not. Through different people, in different voices, we have been giving only one call to the world, and that is of meditation. [8]

Mahakashyapa is known to very few people, because he never wrote and never gave discourses.

One day, Buddha came to his morning discourse with a lotus flower in his hand. He sat silently looking at the flower, not saying a single word. The assembly of ten thousand *sannyasins* was bewildered. This was unheard of! In the first place Buddha, who had never before come with anything, comes with a lotus flower. Secondly, he used to speak immediately, but today minutes and hours have passed, and he is just looking at the flower. Many must have thought he had gone mad. Only one man did not agree — he laughed. That man was Mahakashyapa. Buddha raised his eyes, laughed, and called Mahakashyapa to him.

He gave him the flower and told the assembly that the sermon was over, saying, "I have given to you what you are entitled to, and I have given to Mahakashyapa what he deserves, and rightly so. I have talked to you for years in words, and you have never understood. Today I have spoken in silence, and the laughter of Mahakashyapa has shown that he has understood." In this mysterious way, the successor was found: Mahakashyapa became Buddha's successor. A strange way....

The disciples of Mahakashyapa have written a few things about him which can be called his book. But really neither has he written them, nor have his disciples signed them. They are anonymous, but whatsoever was written is of immense beauty. A few fragments, just like pieces of the full moon...if you can put them together, there will be the full moon again. The secret for putting them together is meditation. The tradition that followed Mahakashyapa is Zen. He is the first patriarch of Zen, of *dhyan*. [9]

the flame of awareness
of awareness

MEDITATION IS A

STATE. YOU ARE

SIMPLY SILENT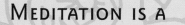

NO THOUGHT

TO CONCENTRATE ON,

NO SUBJECT

TO CONTEMPLATE,

NO OBJECT

TO MEDITATE OVER.

Gorakh is the first link in a chain. From him came the birth of a new type of religion. Without Gorakh, a Kabir could not have happened, nor a Dadu, a Farid, a Meera — without Gorakh none of these would have been possible. After him the temple has been built high. On this temple many golden spires have been raised, and though the golden spires may be seen from afar they cannot be more important than the foundation, which is not visible to anyone. But on these stones stands the whole structure — all the walls, all the high peaks. Though the peaks may be worshipped, people simply forget about the foundation stones. Gorakh is likewise forgotten.... Gorakh made countless discoveries of the inner search, more perhaps than anyone else. He gave so many methods that, in terms of methods, Gorakh is the greatest inventor.... He gave so many methods that people were confused — which method is right, which is wrong, which to do, which to drop.... Gorakh had a rare individuality, like that of Einstein. Einstein gave very penetrating methods for investigating the truth of the universe, such as no one before him had given. Yes, now they can be further developed, now a finer edge can be put on them, but Einstein had done the primary work, the road was first broken by him. Now others will come: the improvers of the road, those who build it up, those who place the milestones, those who beautify it and make it comfortable. But no one can take Einstein's place. In the inner world, the situation is similar with Gorakh. But why have people forgotten

Gorakh? Those who decorated the path are remembered, but the one who first broke the path is forgotten — because those who came later had the leisure to improve it. Whoever comes first will be unpolished, unfinished: Gorakh is like a diamond just out of the mine. If Gorakh and Kabir were sitting together you would be influenced by Kabir, not by Gorakh; because Gorakh is a just-mined diamond and Kabir...on him the jewelers have worked much, he has been well polished.... 🙦 On Gorakh the whole palace of India's Sant literature stands. All is dependent entirely on this one individual. Everything he has said gradually becomes a many-colored splendor. People will do *sadhana*, for centuries they will meditate; who knows how many enlightened beings will be born through it? 🙦 *Die, O yogi, die! Die, sweet is dying.* 🙦 Gorakh says, "I teach death, the death I passed through when I became awakened. It was the death of sleep, not of me. The ego died, not me: duality died, not me. Duality died, and oneness was born. Time died, and I met the eternal. The small constricted life broke, and the drop became the ocean." 🙦 Yes, when the drop falls into the ocean it is certainly dying in one sense, it is dying as a drop. And in another sense the drop attains for the first time to the great life — it lives as the ocean.... Dissolve, die — then comes the divine manifestation, the union. Disappear, then the search is fulfilled and a new expression arises from inside you....

Within the crown of the head a child speaks — how can that be named?

In the crown of the head where the thousand-petaled lotus blooms, no-mind is born. When all thoughts depart, when the ego departs, when even the feeling "I am" does not remain, when the only thing remaining is silence, peace, emptiness — this is called *samadhi*. [10]

The East has been heart-oriented; the West has been mind-oriented. The Western mind has been able to create a great scientific edifice but the Eastern mind could not. How can you create a science from innocence? – it is impossible. So the East has been living unscientifically.

But the West has never been able to know what meditation is. At the most they could pray, but to pray is not the point. You can only pray with the mind; you can go on repeating formulas. If there is no mind, prayer will be silent. You will not be able to pray, there will be no words. With the heart, you can only be prayerful.

In the West they could not develop a spiritual science, they could not develop meditation. They converted meditation into either concentration or contemplation – it is neither – and thereby missed the point. Concentration is a mental process. When the mind is concentrated and the whole thought process is focused, it becomes thinking. It is not a question of the heart.

Meditation is neither contemplation nor concentration. It is
a non-mental, no-mind living. It is to be in contact with the
world with no mind in between. The moment mind is absent,
there is no barrier between you and existence, between you
and the divine; because the heart cannot draw boundaries,
it cannot define.

By defining things, the mind creates barriers, boundaries,
frontiers. But with the heart, existence becomes frontierless.
You end nowhere, and no one else begins anywhere. You are
everywhere, one with the whole of existence....
The master-disciple relationship is an understanding of
the heart. [11]

∾

The East has so many secret keys, but even a single key is
enough because a single key can open thousands and thousands of locks. The relationship between master and disciple
is one such key. [12]

Saraha's original name was "Rahul," the name given to him by his father. We will come to know how he became Saraha — that is a beautiful story. When he went to Sri Kirti, the first thing Sri Kirti told him was: "Forget all your Vedas and all your learning and all that nonsense." It was difficult for Saraha, but he was ready to stake anything. Something in the presence of Sri Kirti had attracted him. Sri Kirti was a great magnet. He dropped all his learning, he became unlearned again.... 🌸 Years passed and, by and by, he erased all that he had known. He became a great meditator. Just the same as he had started to become very famous as a great scholar, now his fame started spreading as a great meditator. People started coming from far and away just to have a glimpse of this young man who had become so innocent, like a fresh leaf, or like dewdrops on the grass in the morning. 🌸 One day while Saraha was meditating, suddenly he saw a vision — a vision that there was a woman in the marketplace who was going to be his real teacher. Sri Kirti has just put him on the way, but the real teaching is to come from a woman. Now, this too has to be understood. It is only Tantra that has never been male chauvinistic. In fact, to go into Tantra you will need the cooperation of a wise woman; without a wise woman you will not be able to enter into the complex world of Tantra. 🌸 He saw a vision: a woman there in the marketplace. So, first a woman. Second — in the marketplace. Tantra thrives in the marketplace, in the thick of life. It is not an attitude of negation; it is utter positivity.

He stood up. Sri Kirti asked him, "Where are you going?" And he said, "You have shown me the path. You took my learning away. You have done half the work — you have cleaned my slate. Now I am ready to do the other half." With the blessings of Sri Kirti who was laughing, he went away. ❧ He went to the marketplace. He was surprised: he really found the woman that he had seen in the vision. The woman was making an arrow; she was an arrowsmith woman. ❧ The third thing to be remembered about Tantra: it says the more cultured, the more civilized a person, the less is the possibility of his Tantric transformation. The less civilized, the more primitive, the more alive a person is. The more you become civilized, the more you become plastic — you become artificial, you become too much cultivated, you lose your roots into the earth. You are afraid of the muddy world. You start living away from the world; you start posing yourself as though you are not of the world. Tantra says: To find the real person you will have to go to the roots.... ❧ An arrowsmith woman is a low-caste woman, and for Saraha — a learned brahmin, a famous brahmin, who had belonged to the court of the king — going to an arrowsmith woman is symbolic. The learned has to go to the vital. The plastic has to go to the real. ❧ He saw this woman, young woman, very alive, radiant with life, cutting an arrow-shaft, looking neither to the right nor to the left, but wholly absorbed in making the arrow. He immediately felt something extraordinary in her presence, something that he had never come across. Even Sri Kirti, his master, paled before the presence of this woman. Something so fresh and something from the very source.... ❧ Saraha watched carefully: The arrow ready, the woman closing one eye and opening the other, assumed the posture of aiming at an invisible target. Saraha came still closer. Now, there was no target; she was simply posing. She had closed one eye, her other eye was open, and she was aiming at some unknown target — invisible, it was not there. Saraha started feeling some message. This posture was symbolic, he felt, but still it was very dim and dark. He could feel something there, but he could not figure it out, what it was. So he asked the woman whether she was a professional arrowsmith, and the woman laughed loudly, a wild laugh, and said, "You stupid brahmin! You have left the Vedas, but now you are worshipping Buddha's sayings, *Dhammapada*. So what is the point? You have changed your books, you have changed your philosophy, but you remain all the time the same stupid man." ❧ Saraha was shocked. Nobody had talked to him that way; only an uncultured woman can talk that way. And the way she laughed was so uncivilized, so primitive — but still, something was very much alive. And he was feeling pulled. She was a great magnet and he was nothing but a piece of iron. ❧ And then she said, "You think you are a Buddhist?" He must have been in the robe of the Buddhist monk, the yellow robe. And she laughed again. And she said, "Buddha's meaning can only be known through actions, not through words and not through books. Is not enough enough for you? Are you not yet fed up with all this? Do not waste any more time in that futile search. Come and follow me!" ❧ And something happened, something like a communion. He had never felt like that before. In that moment, the spiritual significance of what she was doing dawned upon Saraha. Neither looking to the left, nor looking to the right, he had seen her — just looking in the middle. ❧ For the first time he understood what Buddha means by being in the middle: avoid the axis. First he was a philosopher, now he has become anti-philosopher — from one extreme to another. First he was worshipping one thing, now he is worshipping just the opposite — but the worship continues. You can move from the left to the right, from the right to the left, but that is not going to help. You will be like a pendulum moving from the left to the right, from the right to the left.... ❧ He had heard it said so many times by Sri Kirti; he had read about it, he had pondered, contemplated over it; he had argued with others about it, that to be in the middle is the right thing. For the first time he had seen it in an action: the woman was not looking to the right and not looking to the left...she was just looking in the middle, focused in the middle. ❧ And she was so utterly absorbed that she was not even looking at Saraha who was standing there watching her. She was so utterly absorbed, she was so totally in the action — that is again a Buddhist message: To be total in action is to be free of action.... ❧ The woman was totally absorbed. That's why she was looking so luminous, she was looking so beautiful. She was an ordinary woman, but the beauty was not of this earth. The beauty came because of total absorption. The beauty came because she was not an extremist. The beauty came because she was in the middle, balanced. Out of balance comes grace. ❧ For the first time Saraha encountered a woman who was not just physically beautiful, who was spiritually beautiful. Naturally, he was surrendered. The surrender happened. Absorbed totally, absorbed in whatsoever she was doing, he understood for the first time: this is what meditation is. Not that you sit for a special period and repeat a mantra, not that you go to the church or to the temple or to the mosque, but to be in life — to go on doing trivial things, but with such absorption that the profundity is revealed in every action. He understood what meditation is for the first time.... ❧ Realizing this, seeing into this woman's actions, and recognizing the truth, the woman called him "Saraha." His name was Rahul; the woman called him Saraha. "Saraha" is a beautiful word. It means "he who has shot the arrow";

"sara" means "arrow," "ha(n)" means "have shot." "Saraha" means "one who has shot the arrow." The moment he recognized the significance of the woman's actions, those symbolic gestures, the moment he could read and decode what the woman was trying to give, what the woman was trying to show, the woman was tremendously happy. She danced and called him "Saraha," and said, "Now, from today, you will be called Saraha: you have shot the arrow. Understanding the significance of my actions, you have penetrated." Rahul became Saraha. ❧ The legend has it that the woman was nobody but a hidden buddha. The name of the buddha given in the scriptures is Sukhnatha — the buddha who had come to help the great potential man, Saraha. Buddha, a certain buddha of the name Sukhnatha, took the form of a woman. But why? Why the form of a woman? Because Tantra believes that just as a man has to be born out of a woman, so the new birth of a disciple is also going to be out of a woman. In fact, all the masters are more mothers than fathers. They have the quality of the feminine. Buddha is feminine, so is Mahavira, so is Krishna. You can see the feminine grace, the feminine roundness; you can see the feminine beauty; you can look into their eyes and you will not find the male aggressiveness.  So it is very symbolic that a buddha took the form of a woman. Buddhas always take the form of a woman. They may be living in a male body, but they are feminine — because all that is born is born out of the feminine energy. Male energy can trigger it but cannot give birth. A master has to keep you in his womb for months, for years, sometimes for lives.

One never knows when you will be ready to be born. A master has to be a mother. A master has to be tremendously capable of feminine energy, so that he can shower love on you — only then can he destroy. Unless you are certain about his love, you will not allow him to destroy you. How will you trust? Only his love will make you able to trust. And through trust, by and by, he will cut limb by limb. And one day suddenly you will disappear. Slowly, slowly, slowly...and you are gone. *Gate, gate, para gate* — going, going, going, gone. Then the new is born. [13]

In the East we have always defined the ultimate truth as *sat-chit-anand*. "Sat" means truth, "chit" means consciousness, "anand" means bliss. They are all three faces of the same reality. This is the true trinity — not God the Father, and the Son, Jesus Christ, and the Holy Ghost; that is not the true trinity. The true trinity is truth, consciousness, bliss. And they are not separate phenomena, but one energy expressing in three ways, one energy having three faces. Hence in the East we say God is *trimurti* — God has three faces. These are the real faces, not Brahma, Vishnu, Mahesh. Those are for the children — spiritually, metaphysically, for the immature. Brahma, Vishnu, Mahesh: those names are for the beginners.

Truth, consciousness, bliss — these are the ultimate truths. First comes truth; as you enter in, you become aware of your eternal reality: *sat*, truth. As you go deeper into your reality, into your *sat*, into your truth, you become aware of consciousness, a tremendous consciousness. All is light, nothing is dark. All is awareness, nothing is unawareness. You are just a flame of consciousness, not even a shadow of unconsciousness anywhere. And when you enter still deeper, then the ultimate core is bliss — *anand*.

Buddha says: Forego everything that you have thought up to now meaningful, significant. Sacrifice everything for this ultimate because this is the only thing that will make you contented, that will make you fulfilled, that will bring spring to your being...and you will blossom into a thousand and one flowers. [14]

In the East we have another word, *dhyan*. It does not mean concentration, it does not even mean contemplation, it does not even mean meditation. It means a state of no-mind. All those three are mind activities: whether you are concentrating, contemplating, or meditating, you are always objective. There is something you are concentrating upon, there is something you are meditating upon, there is something you are contemplating upon. Your processes may be different but the boundary line is clearcut: it is within the mind. Mind can do all these things without any difficulty. *Dhyan* is beyond mind....

When you use *dhyan*, it does not mean *on* something. It simply means going beyond all objects. You simply are. *Dhyan* is not a process, but a state of being: not a duality between subject and object, but simply a dewdrop slipping from the lotus into the ocean.... Meditation is a state. You are simply silent — no thought to concentrate on, no subject to contemplate, no object to meditate over.... Mind is the barrier. And the more you concentrate, the more you contemplate, the more you meditate upon something, you will never go out of the mind. And mind is the dewdrop I have referred to. So the first thing to understand is that for meditation.... Only in the East and particularly in India was the word first coined. Words are coined only when you have a certain experience which is impossible to express in the existing language.

For ten thousand years India has been pouring all its genius into a single effort, and that is *dhyan*. If you use the word *dhyan*, you will not ask, "On what?" The very word *dhyan* has no intrinsic duality. *Dhyan* means simply silence. Utter silence, serenity. [15]

I am reminded of a story. A woodcutter used to go into the woods every day. Sometimes he had to remain hungry because it was raining; sometimes it was too hot, sometimes it was too cold. ❧ A mystic lived in the woods. He watched the woodcutter growing old, sick, hungry, working hard the whole day. He said, "Listen, why don't you go a little farther?" ❧ The woodcutter said, "What am I going to get a little farther? More wood? Unnecessarily carrying that wood for miles?" ❧ The mystic said, "No. If you go a little farther, you will find a copper mine. You can take the copper into the city, and that will be enough for seven days. You need not come every day to cut the wood." ❧ The man thought, "Why not give it a try?" ❧ He went in and found the mine. And he was so happy...he came back and fell at the feet of the mystic. ❧ The mystic said, "Don't rejoice too much right now. You have to go a little deeper into the woods." ❧ "But," he said, "what is the point? Now I have got seven days' food." ❧ The mystic said, "Still...." ❧ But the man said, "I will lose the copper mine if I go farther." ❧ He said, "You go. You certainly will lose the copper mine, but there is a silver mine. And whatsoever you can bring will be enough for three months." ❧ "The mystic has proved right about the copper mine," the woodcutter thought. "Perhaps he is also right about the silver mine." And he went in and found the silver mine. ❧ And he came dancing and he said, "How can I pay you? My gratitude knows no bounds." ❧ The mystic said, "Don't be in a hurry. Go a little deeper." ❧ He said,

"No! I cannot. I will lose the silver mine." The mystic said, "But there is a gold mine just a few steps deeper." The woodcutter was hesitant. In fact, he was such a poor man, that having a silver mine...he had never dreamed of it. But if the mystic is saying it, who knows? — he may still be right. And he found the gold mine. Now it was enough to come once a year. But the mystic said, "It will be a long time — one year from now you will be coming here and I am getting old — I may not be here, I may be gone. So I have to tell you, don't stop at the gold mine. Just a little more...." But the man said, "Why? What is the point? You show me one thing, and the moment I get it, you immediately tell me to drop that and to go ahead! Now I have found the gold mine!" The mystic said, "But there is a diamond mine just a few feet deeper in the forest." The woodcutter went that very day, and he found it. He brought many diamonds and he said, "This will be enough for my whole life." The mystic said, "Now perhaps we may not meet again, so my last message is: now that you have enough for your whole life, go in! Forget the forest, the copper mine, the silver mine, the gold mine, the diamond mine. Now I give you the ultimate secret, the ultimate treasure that is within you. Your outer needs are fulfilled. Sit the way I am sitting here." The poor man said, "Yes, I was wondering...you know these things — why do you go on sitting here? The question has arisen again and again. And I was just going to ask, 'Why don't you get all those diamonds lying there? Only you know about them. All that gold! Why do you go on sitting under this tree?'" The mystic said, "After finding the diamonds, my master told me, 'Now sit under this tree and go in.'" The man dropped all the diamonds there, and he said, "Perhaps we may not meet again, I don't want to go home — I am going to sit here by your side. Please teach me how to go in, because I am a woodcutter. I know how to go deeper into the woods, but I don't know how to go in." The mystic said, "But all your diamonds, gold, copper, silver — all that will be lost, because all these things are valueless for one who goes in." The woodcutter said, "Don't be bothered about that. You have been right up to now. I trust you, that you will be right in this last stage too."  The function of the master is basically to persuade you by and by to move from the physiology to the psychology; move from the mind to the heart; then move from the heart to the being. [16]

As far back as one can remember, people have gathered around masters, just to sit silently. In the East we call it *darshan*. The West has never understood the meaning of it. It looks stupid, that, "I am going to see the master." Why not have a picture in your house? And okay, go once and see and be finished — but going to see the master every day? Are you mad or something?

The West has never understood that *seeing* — that is the actual meaning of the word *darshan* — means being in the energy field of a man who has come to know himself, to drink out of his well, to look into his eyes, to feel his hands, to listen to his silences, to his words. [17]

It is reported that when Sariputta — one of Gautam Buddha's chief disciples, and one of the few who became enlightened in Gautam Buddha's lifetime — when he came to Gautam Buddha, he had come to argue. He was a well-known teacher, and many thought he was a master. He had come with five thousand disciples to argue with Buddha about the basic principles. Buddha received him with great love and said to both his disciples and Sariputta's disciples, "Here comes a great teacher, and I hope that one day he will become a master." Everybody was puzzled what he meant by it, even Sariputta. Sariputta asked, "What do you mean?" Gautam Buddha said, "You argue well, you are articulate, you are an influential intellectual. You have all the qualities of a genius teacher. You have five thousand very intelligent people as your disciples, but you are not a master yet. If you were a master I would have come to you, you would not have come to me. You are a great philosopher, but you know nothing." "And I trust in your intelligence, that you will not lie: say before all these people that you are a thinker but you have not experienced anything. If you say you have experienced, I am ready to discuss with you. But remember, lying is not going to help. You will be caught immediately, because experience has so many things which are not available in the scriptures. So it is better for you to be clear about it." "I am ready to discuss with you if you say that you have experienced the truth. If you say you have not experienced the truth, I am ready to accept you as my disciple. And I will make you a master, it is a promise — because you are promising. You can choose to lie and discuss with me, or to be true and be a disciple and learn with me, experience with me. And one day when you are a master if you want to discuss with me I will be overjoyed." ❧ For a moment there was immense silence. But Sariputta was really a man of truth. He said, "Buddha is right. I have never thought about it, that he is going to ask about experience. I have been debating around the country, defeating many great so-called teachers, making them my disciples" — that was the rule in India. You discuss, and whoever is defeated becomes a disciple. ❧ So he said, "Many of these disciples were themselves teachers, but nobody ever asked me about experience. I don't have any experience, so there is no question of discussing right now. Right now I touch the feet of Gautam Buddha. And I will wait for the time when I have experienced, when I

am a master myself." ❧ After three years of being with Buddha he became enlightened. He was certainly a very potential case...just on the verge. The day he became enlightened, Buddha called him and asked him, "Do you want to discuss now?" ❧ Sariputta touched Gautam Buddha's feet again and he said, "That time I touched your feet because I had no experience. This time I touch your feet because I have the experience; the question of discussion does not arise. That time it was impossible to discuss; this time too it is impossible to discuss. There is nothing to discuss. I know, you know — and the knowing is the same. And I am your disciple. I may become a master to others, but to you I will always remain a disciple. You have transformed my whole life; otherwise I would have died just arguing unnecessarily, wasting my time and other people's time." [18]

In India, we have divided a man's life into four *ashramas*, or phases of life. This is a scientific experiment that is unique perhaps in the whole history of mankind. If a man's lifespan is one hundred years, it is divided into four phases of twenty-five years each. The first twenty-five years is called *brahmacharyashrama*. In this time, a person's aim was to create and accumulate energy so that when he became a *grihastha*, a householder, then he would be ready to experience deeply all the pleasures of life.

These Indian sages were very daring and courageous people; they were not escapists. The first period of twenty-five years was for the accumulation of enough energy so that during the second period he would be able to touch the peaks and the depths of worldly life, to live life to the optimum. The sages knew this truth: you become free of any desire only if you have experienced it totally. Even if you want to be free of negativity, you will have to live it totally. If something is only partially known the mind continues in the desire to know the remaining part, even if only out of curiosity.

Mulla Nasruddin was on his deathbed and the priest had arrived to perform the last rites. He asked Mulla, "Have you repented all your sins?" Mulla opened his eyes and said, "I am repenting! But there is a slight difference between what you are asking me to do and what I am doing — I am repenting the sins that I have not been able to commit! There has been great anguish in my mind, that who knows what I would have gained if I had committed those sins! Whatever I have done has not brought me anything, but is it certain that, if I had done what I was not supposed to do, that this too would not have brought me anything?"

He felt that he did not gain anything from what he had done, but he thought that perhaps the treasures were hidden in what he had not done. And who could assure him that it was not so?

When Nasruddin was one hundred years old, he celebrated his centenary. The news reporters approached and they asked him, "If you had your life to live again, would you commit the same mistakes again?"

Nasruddin said, "I would definitely make those mistakes, but I would also make all the others that I was not able to make. That is the only change I would make. In this life, I began making mistakes very late in life. If I were to live my life all over again, I would get an earlier start."

Then the reporters asked him, "What is the secret of your long life?" Nasruddin said, "I did not drink until I was ten years old, I did not smoke until then, and I did not touch a girl also until I was ten years old. Except for this, I don't see any other secret for my long life. But if I had another life, I would begin to make those mistakes even a little earlier."

A man regrets the experiences that he could not live. You don't long for the experiences that you have already lived; only the desire for those experiences that you could not enjoy lingers with you.

The Indian sages were intelligent, very wise; they said: Accumulate energy until the age of twenty-five. Let the energy be stored so that when you move into the pleasures of life, you are so much charged with energy that you can dive to the very rock-bottom of the passions. Only then you can see everything that the world can show you. And when it is time to turn your back on that life you will not feel any regrets, you will not be looking back on it. This is the meaning of *brahmacharyashrama*. Its meaning was not that people had to be turned into saints and for that reason they should practice celibacy, no. They are saying that a person should experience the pleasures of life so totally that the futility of it will become absolutely clear to him. Only then, the real saintliness is born.

After this twenty-five-year period of *brahmacharyashrama*, the person then can begin to live the *grihasthashrama*, the worldly life. It was really strange that for the first twenty-five years people were carefully kept away from the world of passions, and then in the next twenty-five years were sent into the world of passions, and with much, much celebration. These were very intelligent people who devised this system. They understood that first energy has to gather and accumulate.

Today, in both the East and the West, there are very few people who are really sexually contented, although sex is more open and readily available than it has ever been in the past. Still, very few people are sexually fulfilled. The reason for this is that even before the energy and strength for sex is allowed to accumulate it is already dissipated. Before the fruit ripens, the roots begin to lose their nourishing juices. The fruit is not allowed to really ripen. Fruits that are unripe cannot fall from the tree, but ripe fruits drop naturally; even the tree does not know when they have fallen. For the fruit to ripen nourishment is necessary, and for life experiences to mature much energy is needed.

This is why, for the first twenty-five years of life, everything is designed for creating and accumulating energy. Every human being can become a reservoir of energy that vibrates because of its own accumulated strength, so he can approach the world with the full potential of his energy. Remember, the more powerful a person is, the sooner he will be free of desires; the weaker he is, the longer it will take — because a weak person cannot experience his passions totally, so naturally he cannot become free of them. What is not totally known and experienced cannot be let go of. A totality of experience is necessary to become free of anything. Until the world can again accept these well-conceived divisions of man's life, it will not be possible for man to become free of his passions.

The sage says that study during the first period of life and experience of life during the second period brings a man to the age of about fifty, when it is time for his children to complete their studies. His child will be about twenty-five years old, and if he is married and beginning to enjoy the world, and the father too goes on producing children, it will look ridiculous. If the father continues to indulge his passions when it is time for his children to indulge theirs, how can this father still expect his children to respect him? How can he then expect respect and trust from his children?

No, the tradition was that on the day that the children come home and get married, the parents move into *vanaprasthashrama*, the third phase; now the whole game is over for them. When the children have entered the phase of indulgence, the parents should naturally be moving into the phase of renunciation. Otherwise, there is no difference between the parents and the children.

At the age of fifty years a person will become *vanaprastha*, meaning: one who has turned his face towards the forest. He does not actually go to the forest yet because his children, who have returned home after their studies, need to be guided and given the benefit of the father's life experiences. That is the father's responsibility. If at this stage the father escapes to the forest, the transfer of knowledge from one generation to the next will not be possible. At this time, the children have just returned fresh from their teacher's house. They have learned words and scriptures and have come back full of energy and enthusiasm about life. They have just returned with all their youthful energy; now it is needed for the father to teach and give guidance about what he has learned during his twenty-five-year period of family life. The father and mother will have their vision turned towards the forest, with their backs towards family life, but they will guide their children for twenty-five years more so that what they know can be passed on.

When the parents become seventy-five years old, the children's children will be returning from their teacher's house. Now it is not necessary for the grandparent to wait anymore: his child, who has become fifty years old, will now take over. His child is now a mature, experienced person, and will begin to transfer his experiences to his own children. Now is the moment for the grandparent to take *sannyas* and go into the forest, deep in his spiritual search. In this way a beautiful circle is created. [19]

Old age has its own dignity. If a person becomes truly mature, old age has its own beauty — which can never be found in a young person. In youth there is excitement but there is no serenity, no coolness of the moon in it. There is great hurry in youth. Hurry is always ugly, it has no beauty. Beauty is like a slowly flowing river, and youth is so full of energy that there is a great impatience to use it.

Youth can never be mentally stable. You say that young people are very healthy, but this health is of the physical body. Mentally, youth is in a very restless state. In that sense, only old people can be mentally at peace — but then only if they become truly mature. Becoming truly mature means that, within the mind, youthful desires do not continue to move and harass you. Otherwise, the body grows old but the mind remains young. This is when old people look very ugly — when their bodies are old and their minds are still full of restlessness and impatience.

It is interesting that children look beautiful, youth looks beautiful, but the old have stopped looking so beautiful. It is difficult to find an old man who looks beautiful. Rabindranath Tagore has said: When an old man, through a full experience of life, ripens to the beauty of old age, then his white hair is like the frozen snow on the peaks of the Himalayas — quiet and peaceful, at the pinnacle, almost touching the sky; where the clouds also bow down in respect. We have called such old people *gurus*, masters or teachers. [20]

When one is finished with happiness, unhappiness, and the duality of it, when one has had enough of it, then the journey for bliss starts, then one starts seeking and searching for something eternal, something deathless. That's what has created *sannyas* in the East. The East is far more ancient than the West. The West is still young, hence still interested in the happiness-unhappiness game. The East is too ancient for that, it has known all those games and the futility of it. *Sannyas* is the greatest contribution of Eastern consciousness to humanity. [21]

golden spires of consciousness

THE EAST HAS SO

MANY SECRET KEYS,

BUT EVEN A SINGLE

KEY IS ENOUGH

BECAUSE A SINGLE

KEY CAN OPEN

THOUSANDS AND

THOUSANDS OF

LOCKS.

India is the only country in the world that has valued a *bhikshu* even more than an emperor. A phenomenon like this is not found anywhere else in the world; it is other-worldly. On this earth nobody has been considered higher than an emperor. India is the only country where we have given a higher place to a *bhikshu* than to an emperor.

An emperor is at the peak of sensual pleasure while a *bhikshu* is at the height of renunciation. An emperor has been collecting things, he has been collecting things like a madman; whereas a *bhikshu* has not saved anything else but himself. An emperor is collecting worldly things while a *bhikshu* is concerned only with his soul. An emperor is lost in worldly things, a *bhikshu* is freeing himself from things so he can enter within himself. An emperor is after worldly pursuits, the *bhikshu* is on his inner journey....

Who is a *bhikshu*? – one who has really become a master. But the real ownership can only be of oneself, it has nothing to do with anybody else. And as long as one tries to enslave another, he is wasting his life. That energy is going to waste, it is not going to serve any purpose. He will not reach anywhere, he will simply drain himself, exhaust himself, finish himself; he will destroy himself....

Mahavira's way is diametrically opposite: you drop the idea of becoming a master on the outside. There is a world within, there is an empire within, a vastness, a sky – you are its master. You claim ownership of that. [22]

I am reminded of one of the greatest emperors, perhaps in the whole of world history. He was Ashoka. He could have become a world conqueror far more easily than Alexander the Great. He had far bigger armies, far more developed technology, far more riches. And he was on the way to becoming a world conqueror, but the first victory was enough. He conquered what is now the state of Orissa. In his days it was called the land of Kalinga. He conquered the country of Kalinga. Millions of people had to be killed, massacred, because the people of that place were ready to die but not to be conquered. The situation was such that the fight would continue until not a single man remained and Ashoka would be victorious only over millions of corpses. Halfway, Ashoka trembled, seeing millions of people massacred, and seeing the point that these are not the people who are going to give way: either life in freedom, or death — there is no other alternative for them. They will not accept any kind of slavery. When he became absolutely certain of it, he thought for a moment — just in the middle of millions of corpses — "Is it worthwhile? What will be the point? Killing these brave people and just becoming victorious over a country of the dead.... You will feel repentant your whole life, because you have destroyed so much life. And not the life of ordinary people, but people of tremendous courage, who have given you absolute alternatives: 'Either we will live in freedom or we will die in freedom. Slavery is not acceptable. You may be a great king, you may have great power, but we have at least the power to die — you cannot take it away from us.'" ❧ The country was poor. It was not in any way comparable to the vast empire of Ashoka. Ashoka's empire was the biggest India has ever seen — from Afghanistan, which is now a separate country, Pakistan, which is now a separate country, Sri Lanka, which is now a separate country, Burma, which is now a separate country, Nepal, Bhutan, Sikkim, Ladakh...India has never had so big a map as it had in the time of Ashoka. ❧ Just this small country of Kalinga was independent, and they were poor. They did not have an army, nor the technology, just courage — such a courage that they had only two simple alternatives: "We will live in freedom or we will die in freedom; we don't know any other alternative." ❧ In fact, Ashoka had become challenged in a way — he had to see how these people for centuries had been free without an army, with just human courage and dignity and pride. It was a great challenge to the great emperor, who could have crushed them without any effort. He had already killed half of the country. ❧ But then suddenly a turn came to his own consciousness,

and he saw that this was simply being stupid: "You are destroying a beautiful, proud people and you are able to destroy because you have bigger armies, you have more weapons, you have better horses, better weapons, but you don't have better human beings than you are destroying. Your people are simply servants who are fighting because they are being paid. These people are fighting without arms, without horses, just because they love freedom. It is ugly to destroy these people — this will be destroying a beautiful variety." ❧ He returned home. His generals asked, "What is the matter? We are winning." ❧ Ashoka said, "This is not victory, this is simply murder. And I am not a murderer. If I cannot conquer them alive, I don't want to conquer. I don't want to be called in history a conqueror of corpses. Forget about it." ❧ And the whole thing became such a nightmare in the mind of Ashoka that the moment he reached his palace he came to a transformation point: he renounced the empire. He said, "Of what use is this whole empire? Enough of it! I don't want any conquering or anybody to conquer, anybody to invade, and I don't want any empire." ❧ Ashoka became a disciple of Gautam Buddha. Gautam Buddha had died two hundred years before, but his disciples were alive, his enlightened disciples were still there. It may have been the third or fourth generation, but there were people who had the same flavor and the same charisma, the same magic.  Ashoka became a disciple, renounced the world, started living like a beggar in his own capital, begging for his food every day in his own capital. [23]

In search of the undivided being, the Eastern mind has tried to find out what exactly is this inner consciousness that the Eastern mystics, saints and sages have been talking about – and calling the body illusory.

To us, the body seems to be real and consciousness is just a word. But because all the saints in the East were insisting that this word "consciousness" is your reality, the East has tried to find out what this reality is before deciding in favor of the body.

The natural tendency will be to decide in favor of the body, because the body is there, already appearing as real; consciousness you have to search for, you have to go on an inner pilgrimage. Because of people like Gautam Buddha and Mahavira, the East could not deny that these people were sincere. Their sincerity was so clear, their presence was so impressive, their words were so authoritative...it was impossible to deny. No argument was enough, because these people were their own argument, their own validity.

And they were so peaceful and so joyful, so relaxed, so fearless. They had everything that every human being desires...and in a way, they had nothing. Certainly they had found a source within themselves, a treasure. And you cannot just deny it without first having given enough time to the search. Unless you find that there is no consciousness, you cannot deny it. We have had people so fragrant...we could not see their roses, but the fragrance was so much that the East tried to look inside, and has found that the soul is far more real and the body is just an appearance. And just by the way, it will be significant to remind you that modern science has also come to the conclusion that matter is illusory, that matter does not exist; it only appears to exist. [24]

In the East it has been a long tradition, one of the ancientmost traditions. When Westerners come to the East they cannot understand what is happening. In India or in Iran or in Arabia, people travel thousands of miles to see a master, just to see a master. They will not ask a single question, they will simply come. And it is a long, arduous journey. Sometimes people will travel on foot for thousands of miles just to have a glimpse of the master.

The Western mind cannot understand what the point is. If you don't have anything to ask, why are you going? For what? The Western mind understands how to converse, but it has forgotten how to be with. It knows how to ask, but it has forgotten how to drink. It knows the intellectual approach, it does not know the door of the heart – that there is a way to connect and to relate beyond words, that there is a way to participate beyond words. So Westerners have always been puzzled about Eastern people walking thousands of miles, making a long, arduous journey, sometimes dangerous, and then coming to a master just to touch his feet and ask for his blessings. And then they will go away fulfilled, happy....

For centuries the East has known a different kind, a different quality, of communication — it is of communion. A man will come, he will touch the feet, he will bow down, he will look at the master, he will just sniff the air around the master — just the fragrance — and he feels fulfilled. He has come to see that the impossible happens. He has heard that it happened in Buddha's time, he has heard that it happened in Mohammed's time, he has heard about great masters like Abdul-Aziz, he has heard great stories — and he wants to see whether it still happens, whether a buddha is still alive, whether he can find a man of the quality of Mohammed so that the scriptures will become valid again. Each master goes on revalidating, each master is again and again a witness to the eternal truth: that truth can be realized.

In the East people travel. They make faraway journeys just to see with their own eyes — because you cannot see Buddha now. Twenty-five hundred years have passed; it is past, it is part of history, you can only read about it. You cannot see Krishna now, he is myth. In the East people want to see somebody who is a Krishna or a Buddha or a Mohammed or a Christ. They want to look into those eyes so that they can again become confident, so that they can again gain trust that it still happens, that God has not forsaken the world yet, that it is not just a story of the past, that it is part of reality. [25]

And there is a great and urgent need to do something that you have never done before: a search for your own self. You have run after everything in the world and it has not led anywhere. All roads in the world go round and round; they never reach any goal. They don't have any goal.

Visualizing this long perspective, one suddenly becomes sick of the whole action — love affairs, fights, anger, greed, jealousy. And one starts thinking for the first time, "Now I should find a new dimension in which I will not be running after anybody, in which I will be coming back home. I have gone too far away in these millions of lives."

This is the foundation of the Eastern wisdom. It creates a great boredom with life, death and the continuous vicious circle. That is the original meaning of the word *samsara*; it means the wheel that goes on moving on, and on, it knows no stopping. You can jump out of it — but you are clinging to it.

This is the basic device to bring you to your senses. You have fooled around enough. Now stop it, and do something that you have been avoiding for centuries, that you have been postponing for tomorrow. [26]

In Buddha's time there was one very beautiful woman and she was a prostitute, her name was Amrapali.... There was always a queue in front of her palace, of kings, princes, the super-rich. It was very difficult to get permission to enter her palace. She was a singer, a musician, a dancer. 🌸 In the East, the meaning of the prostitute is different from in the West. In the West she is simply a sexual object. One goes to a prostitute — that means one goes to a woman as an object, a commodity. A man pays for his sexual pleasure. 🌸 In the East the prostitute is not just an object of sex; in fact, it is not easy to persuade a prostitute to be an object of sex. Particularly in the past that was so.... 🌸 These princes and these kings and these super-rich people all hankered — and they were beautiful people — to somehow persuade Amrapali to be their queen, their wife. But she fell in love with Gautam Buddha. 🌸 Buddha was coming to the city of Vaishali where Amrapali lived. Everybody who was of any significance had gone to receive him. The king was there, the prime minister was there; Amrapali was also there in her golden chariot. Seeing Buddha...she had seen so many beautiful people in her life, but she had never see such a man — so silent, so serene, so peaceful, so relaxed, so at home.... The way he walked — because he came walking, he used to move only on his feet — the way he walked into the city, the grace that surrounded him.... 🌸 Amrapali fell at Buddha's feet and said, "Initiate me as your disciple, give me *sannyas*." 🌸 The prime minister, the king and the princes, and all the so-called big shots could not believe their eyes! Buddha said to Amrapali, "It is better, Amrapali, that you think about it. You are young, you are beautiful. So many people have been waiting for you, they are ready to give you everything you want. You have not looked at any of them. I am a poor man, a beggar, and becoming my disciple means becoming a beggar. You think twice. It is a difficult life. We eat only one time a day, we travel on our feet — just look at my feet. You think again." 🙏 It is said that even Buddha felt sorry to give this woman *sannyas* because she had lived in such luxury, she was such a flower. But Amrapali said to him, "Yes, so many people are waiting for me, but I was waiting for you. And I don't want what they want to give me. They can give me the whole world, but I don't want that. I would love just to follow you in the dusty roads, with naked feet.

I will be immensely happy just to eat food once a day. I am ready to be a beggar. Just to be under your shadow is enough." 🙏 Amrapali was a pagan; she had lived very instinctively. Buddha gave her *sannyas*, but gave her no guidelines. That is the most important thing. He gave *sannyas* to thousands of people but Amrapali was the only exception: to her no principle was given, no guidelines. 🙏 Buddha said, "You go on following the way — you are on the right path. If you had not been on the right path you would not have chosen me. I have got nothing; on the other side is the whole world, and you chose me. That's indication enough that up to now you have been on the right path. Now don't ask for any guidance — that will be a distraction. You simply go on following your own innermost being." 🙏 And Amrapali became enlightened that day. 27

Buddha called his *sannyasins bhikshu* — in Pali, *bhikkhu* — he was mocking us. This is ironical, and he said it only as a joke, but the joke is deep and serious.

Buddha went to a village with his begging bowl to beg, and the wealthiest man of the village said, "Why? Such a beautiful man like you" — at that time Buddha's whole body was so beautiful; perhaps it was difficult to find another man as beautiful as him — "and you are on the road with your begging bowl. You are worthy of being an emperor. I don't care who you are, what you are, what is your caste, your religion, your family. I will marry my daughter to you, and you will become the owner of all my riches because my daughter is my only heir."

Buddha said, "I wish it were true that I am the beggar and you are the emperor. But the fact is that when I saw that you are all beggars thinking you are masters, I took the begging bowl in my own hands. Seeing the situation, it did not feel right for me to call myself a master. You all call yourselves masters, and we are happy to call ourselves beggars! Because in a world where the beggars think they are the masters, it is right for the masters to show themselves as beggars."

It was a rare phenomenon that had happened.
There have been very few emperors born
on the earth who were so great that they
dared to become beggars. And India is the only
country — all alone on the earth — where men like Buddha
and Mahavira went out on the roads to beg. But it is indicative
of an inner mastery — and it is a great joke on us all...great
sarcasm!

Those who are carrying only begging bowls inside, are living
under the illusion that they are masters, and those whose
desires and ambitions have disappeared, they come out
on the roads with begging bowls. What drama! It is a very
interesting irony. But we are unable to understand the ironies
of people like Buddha — this is the trouble. [28]

For centuries, India has been the symbol of the inner journey. It is not just a political entity, it is a spiritual phenomenon. As far back as we know, people have been coming to India from all over the world in search of themselves. Something is in the very climate, something is in the very vibe, that helps....

I went around the world and I could see the difference. Perhaps, because for thousands of years the Eastern genius has been consistently in search of the soul, it has created a certain atmosphere. If you meditate in the East, it seems as if everything helps: the trees, the earth, the air. If you are meditating in America you have to meditate alone — there is no help coming from anywhere. [29]

I am reminded.... In the life of Mahavira, the most important Jaina philosopher.... He is going from one village to another village with his close disciple, Goshalak. And this is the question they are discussing: Mahavira is insisting, "Your responsibility towards existence shows how much you have attained to your authentic reality. We cannot see your authentic reality but we can see your responsibility."  As they are walking, they come across a small plant. And Goshalak is a logician — he pulls the plant and throws it away. It was a small plant with small roots. Mahavira said, "This is irresponsibility. But you cannot do anything against existence. You can try, but it is going to backfire." Goshalak said, "What can existence do to me? I have pulled this plant; now existence cannot bring it to life again." Mahavira laughed. They went into the town, they were going to beg for their food. After taking food, they were coming back, and they were surprised: the plant was rooted again. While they were in the town it had started raining, and the roots of the plant, finding the support of the rain, went back into the soil. They were small roots, it was windy, and the wind helped the plant to stand up again. By the time they had come back, the plant was back to its normal position. Mahavira said, "Look at the plant. I told you you cannot do anything against existence. You can try, but that will turn against you, because that will go on separating you from existence. It will not bring you closer." "Just see that plant. Nobody could have imagined that this will happen, that the rain and the wind together will manage that small plant back, rooted into the earth. It is going to live its life." ❦ "It seems to us a small plant but it is part of a vast universe, a vast existence, of the greatest power there is." And Mahavira said to Goshalak, "From this point our paths separate. I cannot allow a man to live with me who is against existence and feels no responsibility." ❦ Mahavira's whole philosophy of nonviolence can be better expressed as the philosophy of reverence for existence. Nonviolence is simply a part of it. ❦ It will go on happening: the more you find yourself, the more you will find yourself responsible for many things you have never cared about before. Let that be a criterion: the more you find yourself responsible for people, things, existence, the more you can be at ease that you are moving on the right track. [30]

This is something very essential to understand: when a person like Mahavira became nude, it was not a practice; he had not practiced it. He was a king. He distributed all his property, land, money; whatsoever he had, he distributed it all to the masses, to the people. With just a shawl around him he left town. But when he was just leaving the town, he met a beggar who was crippled, who was trying to come to the town because he had heard that Mahavira was distributing things. But he was crippled, so he was just dragging himself, without legs. And he was late, so he met Mahavira when Mahavira was getting out of the city. ❦ He said, "I was coming, but I am without legs so I could not reach in time. You are leaving, and the poorest man of your kingdom has not received anything." ❦ Now Mahavira said, "I have not got anything else except this shawl, but it is very precious, studded with diamonds." So he tore half and gave half to the beggar. He said, "This will be enough for your whole life and I will manage with the other half." So now it remained just like a towel wrapped around him. As Mahavira was entering the forest, a rosebush caught hold of the half that was his shawl. He suddenly found himself naked. He thought to take the shawl back from the rosebush, but then he thought, "What is the point? Sooner or later I am going to lose this shawl. It is so precious that even while I am asleep I will have to take care of it. It is better the rosebush has taken its share and freed me completely. Now I have nothing to fear — nothing can be stolen. And I am left exactly as I was born." This is not practice, this is simple understanding. [31]

Yoga is pure science, and Patanjali is the greatest name as far as the world of yoga is concerned. This man is rare. There is no other name comparable to Patanjali. For the first time in the history of humanity, religion was brought to the state of a science. He made religion a science of bare laws. No belief is needed.

Patanjali is like an Einstein in the world of buddhas. He is a phenomenon. He has the same attitude, the same approach as a rigorous scientific mind. He is not a poet like Krishna. He is not a moralist like Mahavira. Patanjali is basically a scientist thinking in terms of laws. He has come to deduce the absolute laws of the human being, the ultimate working structure of the human mind and of reality.

If you follow Patanjali, you will come to know that he is as exact as any mathematical formula. Simply do what he says and the result will happen. The result is bound to happen; it is just like two plus two equals four. It is just like when you heat water up to one hundred degrees and it evaporates. No belief is needed. You simply do it and know. That is why I say that there is no comparison. On this earth, there has never existed another man like Patanjali. [32]

There is a beautiful story about a great woman mystic of India, Meera. She was really a mad devotee, a mad *bhakta* in tremendous love and ecstasy with God. She was a queen, but she started dancing on the streets. The family disowned her. The family tried to poison her — the family itself — because it was a disgrace for the royal family. The husband was feeling embarrassed, very much embarrassed, and particularly so in those days. And the story belongs to one of the most traditional parts of this country, Rajasthan, where for centuries no one had seen women's faces; they were covered, always covered. Even the husband might not have been able to recognize his wife in the daylight, because they were meeting only in the night, in darkness.  In those days, in such a stupid climate, in such a milieu, the queen started dancing on the streets! Crowds would gather, and she was so drunk with the divine that her sari would slip down, her face would be exposed, her hands would be exposed. And the family was very much perturbed. But she sang beautiful songs, the most beautiful ever sung in the whole world, because they came from her very heart. They were not composed, they were spontaneous outpourings. She was a devotee of Krishna, she loved Krishna. She told her husband, "Don't go on believing that you are my husband; my husband is Krishna. You are not my husband, only a poor substitute." The king was very angry. He expelled her from the kingdom; she was not allowed to enter the territory. She went to Mathura, the place of Krishna.

Krishna had died thousands of years before, but for her he was as alive as ever. That is the mystery of love: it transcends the barriers of time and space. Krishna was not just an idea to her, he was a reality. She talked to him, she slept with him, she hugged him, kissed him. Nobody else could see Krishna, but she was absolutely aware of him. Krishna represented to her the very spirit of existence, what Buddha calls *dhamma*, the law. That is the masculine formation, the masculine expression: the law. Meera calls Krishna "my beloved" – not law, but love; that is the feminine heart. She reached Mathura; there is one of the greatest temples of Krishna. And the head priest of that temple had taken a vow that he would not see any woman in his life; for thirty years he had not seen a woman. No woman was allowed to enter into the temple and he had never left the temple. When Meera reached there, she danced at the gate of the temple. The guards became so enchanted, magnetized, that they forgot to prevent her. She entered into the temple; she was the first woman after thirty years to enter the temple. The head priest was worshipping Krishna. When he saw Meera he could not believe his eyes. He was mad! – he shouted at her, "Get out of here! Woman, get out of here! Don't you know that no woman is allowed here?" Meera laughed and said, "As far as I know, I know that, except God, everybody is a woman – you too. After thirty years of worshipping Krishna, do you think you are still a male?" It opened the eyes of the head priest; he fell at the feet of Meera. He said, "Nobody has said such a thing ever before, but I can see it, I can feel it – it is the truth." At the highest peak, whether you follow the path of love or meditation, you become feminine.... Buddha and Lao Tzu, all these people seem to be feminine, because you know them only when they have reached the highest peak. But you don't know their path, you don't know their journey. Their journey was masculine, it was not feminine. [33]

Among the lovers of Krishna, Chaitanya's name is the most outstanding.  In the term *achintya bhedabhed-avad*, the word "achintya," which means "the unthinkable," is precious. Those who know through thought will say that either matter and spirit are *bhed*, separate, or that they are *abhed*, one and the same. Chaitanya says they are both, one and separate.... But this is still within the realm of thinking; one can mentally work out that the wave and the ocean are both different and the same together. But Chaitanya adds another word to it, another dimension: that is *achintya*, or "unthinkable." And this word is very significant. He says that if you come to know through thinking that the world and God, matter and spirit, are both separate and inseparable, this realization is worth nothing. It is nothing more than an idea, a concept, a theory. But when a seeker comes to it without thinking, without words, when he realizes it in a state of no-mind, beyond thought, then it is his experience. Then it is worthwhile; it is real and great.... When Chaitanya says that this is unthinkable, he is saying more than what meets the eye. Meera might say it is unthinkable, but she was never given to serious thinking — she was through and through a woman of feelings. But as far as Chaitanya is concerned, he was a great logician, renowned for his sharp mind and brilliant logic. He had scaled the highest peaks of thinking. Pundits were afraid of entering into argument with him. He was incomparable as a debater; he had won laurel after laurel in philsophical discussions. ᐧ Such a rational intellect, who had indulged in hair-splitting interpretations of words and concepts throughout his life, was one day found singing and dancing through the streets of Navadeep. Meera, on the other hand, never indulged in pedantry and scriptures; she had nothing to do with logic. She was a loving woman.... ᐧ But Chaitanya was her opposite; he was not a man of love, and yet he turned to love and devotion, which was a miracle. The one-hundred-and-eighty-degree turn in his life demonstrates the victory of love over logic. He had defeated all his contemporaries with his logic, but when he came to himself he found it to be a self-defeating discipline. He came to a point where the mind lost, and life and love won. Beyond this point one can only go with life and love. ᐧ That is why I say that among people who walked the path of Krishna, Chaitanya was simply extraordinary, incomparable.... ᐧ It is unthinkable how a tremendously

logical mind like Chaitanya could come down from his ivory tower, take a drum in his hands, and dance and sing in the marketplace. Can you think of Bertrand Russell dancing through the streets of London? Chaitanya was like Russell — an out-and-out intellectual. And for this reason his statement becomes immensely significant. He makes his statement that reality is unthinkable not with words, but with a drum in his hands — dancing and singing through the streets of his town, where he was held in great respect for his superb scholarship. It is in this way that he renounces mind, renounces thinking and declares, "Reality is beyond thought, it is unthinkable." ᐧ Chaitanya's case demonstrates that they alone can transcend thinking who first enter into the very depth of thinking and explore it through and through. Then they are bound to come to a point where thinking ends and the unthinkable begins. ᐧ This last frontier of mind is where a statement like this is born. [34]

Chaitanya achieved the ultimate through singing and dancing. He achieved through dancing exactly what Mahavira and Buddha achieved through meditation, through stillness.

There are two ways to come to the axle — the center, to the supreme. One way lies in your being so steady and still, that there is not a trace of trembling in you and you arrive at the center. The other way is just the contrary: you get into such terrific motion that the wheel runs at top speed and the axle becomes visible and knowable. And this second way is easier than the first.

It is easy to know the axle if the wheel is in motion. While Mahavira comes to know it through stillness, through meditation, Krishna knows it through dancing. And Chaitanya surpasses even Krishna in dancing; his dance is magnificient, incomparable. Perhaps no other person on this earth danced as much as Chaitanya. In this connection it is good to bear in mind that man has both a circumference and a center, and while his circumference, the body, is always moving and changing, his center — his soul — is still and quiet; it is eternal. [35]

The very concept of *guru* is Eastern; the word cannot even be rightly translated. When we translate it as "master," much of its meaning is lost, because a master means a teacher. The *guru* is not a teacher. In the Western consciousness nothing like the *guru* has ever existed. That phenomenon is Eastern...it is something basically Eastern. It has to be understood.

We call a person "guru" who can impart the truth to you. Not that he can teach – truth cannot be taught, it can be caught. The *guru* is a person whose presence can help you to catch it...a catalytic agent. He is not going to do anything in fact, he is not a doer. In fact, a person becomes a *guru* when he completely loses his "doer-hood" – then he is no longer a doer; when the doer is gone, the ego is gone, when he is absolutely passive, when not even a slight ripple of desire arises. When there is no desire there cannot be any doing – the doing needs desire and the doing needs a doer.

A master or *guru* is a person who is a non-entity, a nobody. But through his nobodyness the infinite starts flowing. Through his emptiness the whole starts flooding. The *guru* is the person in whose presence truth can be caught.

It depends much on the disciple, because the *guru* is not a doer — he is simply there like a flame of light. If you open your eyes, your eyes become full of light. If you keep your eyes closed, the flame is there: but it is not aggressive, it will not even knock on your eyelids — it will not say, "Open your eyes"; it will not say anything. It will be simply there...it will not interfere with you.

If you open your eyes, you become a receiver. If you don't open your eyes, you miss. [36]

Krishna is utterly incomparable. He is so unique, and his first uniqueness lies in the fact that although he happened in the distant past, he belongs to the future. He is really of the future. Man has yet to grow to the heights where he can be a contemporary of Krishna's....

The most important reason is that Krishna is the only great man in our whole history who reached the absolute height and depth of consciousness, and yet he is not at all serious, sad, in tears. By and large, the chief characteristic of a religious person has been that he is somber, serious and sad-looking, like someone defeated in the battle of life, like a runaway from life. In the long line of all the sages, it is Krishna alone who comes dancing, singing and laughing.

Religions of the past were all life-negative and masochistic, teaching that sorrow and suffering are great virtues. A laughing religion, a religion that accepts life in its totality, is yet to be born. And it is good that the old religions are dead, and that along with them the old God, the God of our old concepts, is also dead.
Up to now, every religion has divided life into two parts, and while they accept one part they deny the other. Krishna alone accepts the whole of life. The acceptance of life in its totality has come to its peak in Krishna. [37]

In Maharashtra, there is a temple which is one of the most holy places in India. The temple is called Vithoba temple. Vithoba is one of Krishna's names. The story is that a devotee of Krishna became so deeply meditative that Krishna had to come to him.

When he arrived, the devotee was massaging the feet of his mother. Krishna came and knocked on the door. It was open, so he came in and sat just behind the devotee, who for many lives had been crying and begging Krishna to come to him. Just by turning his head the devotee would be fulfilled; his long effort would come to a fulfillment.
Krishna said, "Look, I am here. Look at me." And the devotee said to him "Wait!" because he had not come at the right moment, he was massaging his mother's feet. He was sitting on a small earthen brick, so he took it out and pushed it back, telling Krishna to sit on it. He never turned to look at him, to welcome and thank him.

Krishna stood on that brick and waited the whole night, because the mother could not go to sleep, she was dying, and the devotee could not leave her. God could wait. The morning came and the town started to wake up. Krishna became worried that others might see him, so he became a statue.

And that statue is there in that temple. Krishna is standing on that brick waiting for the devotee who never turned around! The story is... something. Only in such deep moments of renunciation — not even the desire to see God — and the devotee attained. [38]

Ramakrishna died. In India, whenever a husband dies his wife has to break her bangles, take off all her ornaments, shave her head completely, use only white saris — a lifelong mourning, a lifelong despair, a lifelong loneliness starts. But when Ramakrishna died — and it was just in the past century — his wife, Sharda, refused to follow the ten-thousand-year-old tradition.  She said, "Ramakrishna cannot die — at least for me. He may have died for you; to me it is impossible because to me his physical body became irrelevant long ago. His presence and the experience, the fragrance, have become a reality — and they are still with me. And until they leave me I am not going to break my bangles or cut my hair or do anything, because to me he is still alive." People thought that she had gone mad: "The shock seems to be too much — not a single tear." Even when Ramakrishna's body was taken to the burning place she did not come out of the home. She was preparing food for Ramakrishna. The man was dead — his body had been carried to the crematorium — and she was preparing food because it was his lunch time. And somebody told her, "Sharda, are you mad! They have taken his body away." She laughed and she said, "They have taken his body but they have not taken his presence; that has become part of my being. And I am not mad. In fact by dying he has given me an opportunity to know whether his teaching has entered my heart or not." She lived for many years afterwards, and every day there was the same routine: twice a day she would prepare food, and — as the old Hindu wife sits by the side of the husband while he is eating, fanning him — she would fan an empty seat. Ramakrishna was not there — at least for those who can see only the physical. And she would talk and gossip about what has happened in the neighborhood. She would give all the news the way she always used to give. In the evening, again the meal. At night she would prepare his bed, take care of the mosquito net so that not even a single mosquito was inside, touch his feet — which were only visible for her, for nobody else — put the light off and go to sleep. And in the morning in the same way as she used to wake him up, she would come and say, "Paramahansadeva, get up; it is time. Your disciples are gathering outside and you have to prepare — take a bath, a cup of tea." Slowly slowly the people who were more of the heart, not of the mind, started feeling that there was no symptom of madness in Sharda. On the contrary...because of Ramakrishna they had never thought about her; she was always behind.

But now Ramakrishna was gone, and she was the oldest companion. They started asking her advice, and her advice was so perfect on every matter that it was impossible for her to be mad. But as far as Ramakrishna was concerned, she continued to feel his presence to the last breath of her life. Before dying...that was the only time that she started crying. Somebody said, "You didn't cry when Ramakrishna died. Why are you crying?" She said, "I am crying because now who will take care, who will prepare the food? Nobody knows what he likes, what he does not like. Who will make his bed? And the place is so full of mosquitoes that if the mosquito net is not put rightly, if just a small place is available for mosquitoes to enter, the old man will suffer the whole night — and I am dying. I will not be here. And you all think he is dead, so I cannot rely on you." Now this is the approach of a silent, waiting heart. Even death cannot make any difference, any distance. [39]

It is said about Buddha that when he became enlightened, trees flowered out of season. They may not have flowered; this may not be a scientific statement. But a statement need not be scientific to be true, a statement need not be historical to be true. There are planes and planes of truth. There is a certain quality in a poetic truth also. It is not historic, it is not scientific, but it is true all the same. It is a poetic truth. And a poetic truth is on a higher plane than any scientific truth, because scientific truths go on changing; a poetic truth is eternal. Scientific truth is more or less a fact. A poetic truth is not a fact but a deep significance, a meaning, a myth. [40]

 It is said about Mahavira that when he would walk and move from one village to another — and he was nude, a naked man with no shoes, no clothes — sometimes thorns would be on the path: they would immediately turn to protect his feet. Thorns may not have done this — one cannot expect that much from thorns. Even from human beings it is too much to expect. But still, the idea is significant. It simply shows one thing: that we are members of each other. Thorns are also part of us, and we are part of thorns. Flowers are also part of us, and we are part of flowers. We are one family; we are not strangers, separate islands — a vast continent of being, interrelated. [41]

fragrance
of the
east

THE WHOLE STORY

OF INDIA IS A STORY

OF NONVIOLENCE....

NO OTHER COUNTRY

IN THE WORLD IS

FEMININE IN THE

SAME SENSE AS INDIA.

Enough of scholarship. Scholarship is just very mediocre; scholarship cannot bridge modern science with mysticism. We need buddhas, not people who know about Buddha. We need meditators, lovers, experiencers. And then the day is ripe, the time has come, when science and religion can meet and mingle, can be welded together. And that day will be one of the greatest days of the whole of human history; it will be a great day of rejoicing, incomparable, unique, because from that day, the schizophrenia, the split humanity will disappear from the world. Then we need not have two things, science and religion; one thing will do.

For the outer world it will use scientific methodology, for the inner it will use religious methodology. And "mysticism" is a beautiful word; it can be used for that one science or one religion, whatsoever you call it. "Mysticism" will be a beautiful name. Then science will search for the outer mystery, and religion will search for the inner mystery; they will be the two wings of mysticism. "Mysticism" can become the word that denotes both, mysticism can be the synthesis of both.

And with this synthesis, many more syntheses will happen on their own accord. For example, if science and religion can meet in mysticism, then East and West can meet, then man and woman can meet, then poetry and prose can meet, then logic and love can meet, then layer upon layer, meetings can go on happening. And once this has happened, we will have a more perfect man, more whole, more balanced. [42]

The greatest mystics of the world were often the greatest logicians too. Shankara, Nagarjuna — they were great logicians and yet illogical. They will go as far as possible with logic, and then suddenly they take a quantum leap — they say, "Up to this point, logic helps, beyond this, logic has to go."

If you want to argue with Shankara, you will be defeated. Shankara traveled all over this country, and he defeated thousands of scholars. This was his whole life's work, to go and defeat people. And still he was very illogical. In the morning you would find him arguing so logically that the greatest logicians would look childish. And in the evening you would find him praying and dancing in the temple and crying and weeping like a child. Unbelievable.

He had written one of the most beautiful prayers, and somebody asked, "How can you write such beautiful prayers? You are such a logician — how can you be so emotional that you cry and weep and tears fall down?" He said, "My intuition is not against my logic, my intuition is beyond my logic. My logic has some function to fulfill; I go with it, I go with it wholeheartedly, but then there comes a moment when it cannot go beyond...and I have to go beyond it too." [43]

I will tell you of one incident in Rabindranath Tagore's life. Rabindranath often used to go on his small houseboat and live for months on the beautiful river, surrounded by thick forest, in absolute silence and aloneness.

One full-moon night, it happened that he was reading a very significant contribution to the philosophy of aesthetics, by Croce.... In the middle of night, tired from Croce's very complicated arguments, he closed the book and blew out the candle. He was going to his bed to sleep, but a miracle happened.

As the small flame of the candle disappeared, from every window and door of the small houseboat the moon came dancing in. The moon filled the house with its splendor. Rabindranath remained silent for a moment. It was such a sacred experience. He went out of the house, and the moon was immensely beautiful in that silent night amongst those silent trees, with a river flowing so slowly that there was no noise. He wrote in his diary the next morning, "The beauty was all around me, but a small candle had been preventing it. Because of the light of the candle, the light of the moon could not enter."

This is exactly the meaning of *nirvana*. Your small flame of the ego, your small flame of the mind and its consciousness, is preventing the whole universe from rushing into you; hence the word *nirvana* — blow out the candle and let the whole universe penetrate you from every nook and corner. You will not be a loser. You will find, for the first time, your inexhaustible treasure of beauty, of goodness, of truth — of all that is valuable. [44]

Adi Shankaracharya. He is a predecessor of nearly fourteen hundred years ago. He died as a young man, he died when he was thirty-three. He created a new tradition of *sannyasins*; he created four temples in all the four directions, and he appointed four *shankaracharyas*, one for each direction. I remember about him that he traveled all over the country defeating great, well-known philosophers. That was in a totally different atmosphere. One great philosopher was Mandan Mishra; he had a great following. A town still exists in his memory.... Shankara must have been at the age of thirty when he reached Mandala. Just on the outskirts of the town, by a well, a few women were drawing water. He asked them, "I want to know where the great philosopher Mandan Mishra lives." Those women started giggling and they said, "Don't be worried, you just go inside. You will find it." Shankara said, "How will I find it?" They said, "You will find it, because even the parrots around his house — he has a big garden and there are so many parrots in the garden — they repeat poetry from the Upanishads, from the Vedas. If you hear parrots repeating, singing beautiful poetry from the Upanishads, you can be certain that this is the house of Mandan Mishra." He could not believe it, but when he went and he saw, he had to believe. He asked Mandan Mishra — he was old, nearabout seventy — "I have come a very long way from South India to have a discussion with you, with a conditon: if I am defeated, I will become your disciple, and if you are defeated, you will have to become my disciple. Naturally, when I become your disciple all my disciples will become your disciples and the same will be true if you become my disciple — all your disciples will become my disciples." 🙐 Old Mandan Mishra looked at the young man and he said, "You are too young and I feel a little hesitant whether to accept this challenge or not. But if you are insistent, then there is no way; I have to accept it. But it does not look right that a seventy-year-old man who has fought thousands of debates should be fighting with a young man of thirty. But to balance, I would suggest one thing" — and this was the atmosphere that had a tremendous value — "to compensate, I will give you the chance to choose the judge who will decide. So you find a judge. You are too young, and I feel that if you are defeated at least you should have the satisfaction that the judge was of your choice." 🙐 Now where to find a judge? The young man had heard much about Mandan Mishra's wife. Her name was Bharti. She was also old, sixty-five. He said, "I will choose your wife to be the judge." 🙐 This is the atmosphere, so human, so loving. First Mandan Mishra gave him the chance to choose,

and then Shankara chose Mandan Mishra's wife! And Bharti said, "But this is not right. I'm his wife, and if you are defeated you may think it is because I may have been prejudiced, favorable towards my husband." 🙐 Shankara said, "There is no question of any suspicion. I have heard much about your sincerity. If I'm defeated, I'm defeated. And I know perfectly well if your husband is defeated, you will be the last person to hide the fact." 🙐 Six months it took for the discussion. On each single point that man has thought about they quarreled, argued, quoted, interpreted, and after six months the wife said, "Shankara is declared victorious. Mandan Mishra is defeated." 🙐 Thousands of people were listening for these six months. It was a great experience to listen to these two so-refined logicians, and this was a tremendous experience, that the wife declared Shankara to be the winner. There was great silence for a few moments, and then Bharti said, "But remember that you are only half the winner, because according to the scriptures the wife and husband make one whole. I'm half of Mandan Mishra. You have defeated one half; now you will have to discuss with me." 🙐

Shankara was at a loss. For six months he had tried so hard; many times he had been thinking of giving up — the old man was really very sharp even in his old age. Nobody has been able to stand up against Shankara for six months, and now the wife says his victory is only half. Bharti said, "But I will also give you the chance to choose your judge." ❧ He said, "Where am I going to find a better judge than Mandan Mishra? You are such simple and fair and sincere people." But Bharti was very clever, more clever than Shankara had imagined, because she started asking questions about the science of sex. ❧ Shankara said, "Forgive me, I am a celibate and I don't know anything about sex." ❧ Bharti said, "Then you will have to accept your defeat, or if you want some time to study and experience, I'm willing to give you some time." ❧ He was caught in such a strange situation;

he asked for six months and six months were given. "You can go and learn as much as you can because this will be the subject to begin with, then later on other subjects. It is not easy," Bharti said, "to beat Mandan Mishra. But that half was easier! I am a much harder woman. If I can declare the defeat of my husband, you can understand that I am a hard woman. It is not going to be easy. If you feel afraid don't come back; otherwise we will wait for six months." ❧ This atmosphere continued for thousands of years. There was no question of being angry, there was no question of being abusive, there was no question of trying to prove that you are right by your physical strength or by your arms or by your armies — these were thought to be barbarous methods, these were not for cultured people. 45

In the future, minds who have known something of meditation, reading about the past, will be surprised that countries like India — so vast — were so easily conquered.

The credit does not go to the conquerors, remember. The credit goes to the defeated, the conquered — because these people have lived in a totally different atmosphere, a different milieu; they have been nourished on different vibrations. Fighting and killing for the land, for the money, was not in their minds. They were conquered not because they were not brave enough, they were conquered because they were not foolish enough to fight. They allowed the way; they said, "A few idiots have got this idea to conquer the whole world — let them conquer. What are you going to gain by conquering the whole world?" A totally different approach to life: that the very idea of conquering is ugly, inhuman.

But to the Alexanders, to the Napoleons, to the Hitlers, to conquer was the greatest thing in life; there was nothing more. India knows much more. India knows that there is certainly a way of conquering — but it is not concerned with conquering others, it is concerned with conquering oneself. [46]

J am reminded of one great mystic, Nagarjuna. He used to live naked. He had only a begging bowl; that was his only possession. But perhaps he was the greatest genius that has been born on this earth. As far as intelligence is concerned, his sharpness is incomparable. Great kings, queens, great philosophers were his students. One queen was very much devoted to him, and when he came to her capital she had made a golden begging bowl, studded with diamonds. And when he came to the palace to beg, she said, "First you have to give me a promise." He said, "You are asking a promise from a naked man who has nothing but his begging bowl." She said, "That will do. I'm just asking for the begging bowl." He said, "You can take it." She said, "That is only half. I will replace it, and you will have to take my begging bowl." He said, "There is no problem, any begging bowl will do." He was not aware of what she was hiding. It was a golden begging bowl studded with very valuable diamonds." He took it. As he was going back to the ruins of the monastery where he was staying, a thief saw him and could not believe his eyes. The begging bowl was shining like stars. And he is a naked man — of course very beautiful, magnificent, "But what is the begging bowl doing with this naked man? And how long can he keep it? Somebody is going to take it away, so why not I?" He followed Nagarjuna. Nagarjuna went inside a room, which was a little shed with just the walls left. The whole monastery was in ruins, and there was a window in the side, and the thief was hiding outside the window knowing that Buddhist monks eat only once a day. "Now he will eat, and then he will have a little sleep – just a nap – and that will be the right moment. Nobody lives in this monastery. It is thousands of years old." 🐚 Nagarjuna ate his food and threw the bowl out of the window to where the thief was sitting. The thief could not believe it. He was really shocked. For a moment he could not think what to do. "What kind of man is he? – he has eaten his food and thrown away this immensely valuable bowl as if it is of no use, and to exactly where I am sitting." 🐚 He stood up and he asked Nagarjuna, "Can I come in just to ask one question?" 🐚 Nagarjuna said, "To bring you in, I had to throw the bowl out! Come in. The bowl is yours; don't be worried. I have given it to you so you will not be a thief. It is a gift, a present. I am a poor man. I don't have anything else, only that bowl, and I know I cannot keep it for long because I will have to sleep; somebody will take it away, and you have taken so much trouble. You followed me from the capital, and I have been watching. And it is a hot summer day. Please don't refuse. Take it." 🐚 The thief said,

"You are a strange man. Don't you know how costly it is?" 🐚 Nagarjuna said, "Since I have known myself nothing is costly." 🐚 The thief looked at Nagarjuna and said, "Then give me one more present: how can I know myself, which in comparison makes this precious bowl worth nothing?" 🐚 Nagarjuna said, "It is very simple." 🐚 But the thief said, "Before you say anything I want to introduce myself. I am a well-known thief." 🐚 Nagarjuna said, "Who is not? Don't be concerned with trivia. In this world everybody is a thief because everybody comes naked without anything, and then everybody gains something or other. All are thieves, so don't be worried. That's why I live naked. It is perfectly okay. Whatever you are doing, do it well. Just do one thing: when you are stealing be aware, be alert, be watchful. If you lose watchfulness, then don't steal. That is a simple rule for you." 🐚 The thief said, "It is very simple. When can I see you again?" 🐚 Nagarjuna said, "I will be here for two weeks. You can come any day, but first try it." 🐚 For two weeks he tried, and he found that it was the most difficult thing in the world. Once he even reached inside the palace, opened the door of the treasures...but when he would try to take something he would lose his awareness. And he was an honest man. So he would have to leave that thing — that cannot be taken. But it was difficult: when he was aware, there was no desire to take the whole treasure. ✤ Finally he came empty-handed to Nagarjuna and he said, "You have disturbed my whole life. Now I cannot steal." ✤ Nagarjuna said, "That is not my problem. Now it is your problem. If you want to steal, forget all about awareness." ✤ But the thief said, "Those few moments of awareness were so valuable. I have never felt so at ease, so peaceful, so silent, so blissful — the whole treasure of the kingdom was nothing compared to it." ✤ "Now I understand what you mean by saying that once you have known yourself, nothing else is of value. I cannot stop practicing awareness. I have tasted just a few drops of the nectar which you must be tasting every moment. Will you allow me to be a disciple and follow you?" ✤ Nagarjuna said, "I knew it that very day. I had initiated you already when you followed me. You were thinking that you are going to steal the begging bowl, and I was thinking how to steal you. We are both in the same business!" [47]

A very rich man once wanted to become happy. He had tried all kinds of ways but everything had failed. He went to many saints; nobody could help him. Then somebody suggested, "You go to Mulla Nasruddin. He lives in a certain town — he is the only man who can be of some help to you."  The man went with a bag full of diamonds, and he showed the bag to Mulla Nasruddin who was sitting underneath a tree outside the town, resting under the sun. And he said, "I am a very miserable man — I want happiness. I am ready to give anything for it, but I have not tasted even once what happiness is — and death is coming closer. Can you help me? How can I be happy? I have all kinds of things that the world can give to me, yet I am unhappy. Why?" Mulla looked at the man, and it happened so fast that the rich man could not understand what was happening. He just jumped on the man, took away the bag, and ran. Of course the man followed, crying, shouting, "I have been cheated, robbed!" Mulla knew all the streets of the town, so he was going zigzag, this way and that. And the rich man had never run in his life, and he was crying and tears were flowing down, and he said, "I have been robbed absolutely — that was my whole life's earnings. Save me, people! Help me!" And a crowd followed. And by the time they reached Mulla, the Mulla had come back to the place where the rich man had found him. The rich man's horse was still standing there, Mulla was sitting under the tree. The rich man was crying, breathing hard. And Mulla gave the bag back to him.

The rich man said, "Thank God!" And such tears of joy, and such peace. Mulla said, "Look, I have made you happy. Now you know what happiness is? This bag has been with you for years and you were unhappy. It had to be taken away from you." Happiness is part of unhappiness. That's why happiness should not be the goal of your life, because if you want happiness you will have to remain unhappy. The unhappier you are, then only a few moments, few and far between, will be those of happiness. The goal is not happiness, the goal is bliss.... Happiness is worthless: it depends on unhappiness. Bliss is transcendence: one moves beyond the duality of being happy and unhappy. One watches both — happiness comes, one watches and does not become identified with it. One does not say, "I am happy. Peace — it is wonderful." One simply watches, one says, "Yes, a white cloud passing." And then comes unhappiness, and one does not become unhappy either. One says, "A black cloud passing — I am the witness, the watcher." This is what meditation is all about — just becoming a watcher. Failure comes, success comes, you are praised, you are condemned, you are respected, you are insulted — all kinds of things come, they are all dualities. And you go on watching. Watching the duality, a third force arises in you, a third dimension arises in you. The duality means two dimensions — one dimension is happiness, another is unhappiness. Watching both, a depth arises in you — the third dimension, witnessing, *sakshi*. And that third dimension brings bliss. Bliss is without any opposite to it. It is serene, tranquil, cool. It is ecstasy without any excitement. [48]

The Bauls are called Bauls because they are mad people. The word *baul* comes from the Sanskrit root *vatul*, which means "mad, affected by the wind." The Baul belongs to no religion. He is neither Hindu nor Mohammedan nor Christian nor Buddhist. He is a simple human being. His rebellion is total. He does not belong to anybody; he belongs only to himself. He lives in a no-man's land: no country is his, no religion is his, no scripture is his. His rebellion goes even deeper than the rebellion of the Zen masters because, at least formally, they belong to Buddhism, they worship Buddha. Formally, they have scriptures — scriptures denouncing scriptures, of course, but still they have them. At least they have a few scriptures to burn.

Bauls have nothing — no scripture, not even to burn; no church, no temple, no mosque — nothing whatsoever. A Baul is a man always on the road. He has no house, no abode. God is his only abode, and the whole sky is his shelter. He possesses nothing except a poor man's quilt, a small, handmade one-stringed instrument called an *ektara*, and a

small drum, a kettle-drum. That's all that he possesses, just
a musical instrument and a drum. He plays with one hand
on the instrument and he goes on beating the drum with the
other. The drum hangs by the side of his body, and he dances.
That is all of his religion.

Dance is his religion; singing is his worship. He does not even
use the word "god." The Baul word for God is *adhar manush*,
the essential man. He worships man. He says that inside you
and me, inside everybody, there is an essential being.
That essential being is all. To find that *adhar manush*, that
essential man, is the whole search.

So there is no God somewhere outside you, and there is
no need to create any temple because you are his temple
already. The whole search is withinwards. And on the
waves of song and on the waves of dancing, he moves
withinwards. [49]

Gargi lived five thousand years ago, when the Upanishads were being written. It was the childhood of mankind, and man had not yet become so brutal against women. 🦚 Every year the emperor of the nation used to call all the wise people for a contest. He was himself very philosophically-minded. In fact, no enlightened person would have gone to those contests; they were childish, although there was great reward. And it happened one year that the emperor declared that he would give one thousand cows, with their horns covered with pure gold and studded with diamonds, to the person who won the contest. 🦚 Yagnavalkya was one of the most famous and learned men of those days. And he was so confident of his victory that when he came to the campus where the debate was being arranged, he looked at the cows — those one thousand cows with gold-covered horns, studded with diamonds, were looking really beautiful in the sunlight. He told his disciples, "You take these cows to our place. It is unnecessary for the poor cows to stand in the hot sun." 🦚 The disciples said, "But first you have to win." 🦚 He said, "That I will take care of." 🦚 Even the emperor could not prevent him. And all those thousands of wise men who had gathered — they could not prevent him. They all knew that it was impossible to beat him in argument. His disciples took away the cows. 🦚 And it was almost the moment when he was going to be declared the winner, when a woman named Gargi.... She was waiting for her husband who had also gone into the debate, and it

was getting late; so she went herself to call him. She entered the campus and she saw the whole scene – that the cows had been taken away even before victory. 🐚 And she said to the emperor, "Don't declare his victory. Just by chance I had come here to look for my husband...but this man Yagnavalkya needs somebody who really knows, and I am ready to have a discussion with him. He is only a learned man, but learning has never known truth." 🐚 Those were more beautiful days, when even a woman could challenge the most learned man. And the emperor said, "Then I will have to wait. You can discuss." 🐚 She asked only simple questions. She asked, "Who created the world?" And Yagnavalkya laughed, thinking that this woman was asking a childish question. But he was wrong. 🐚 He said, "God created it – because everything that exists has to be created by someone." 🐚 This was the time for Gargi to laugh. She said, "You are caught; now you are in trouble. Who created God? –

because he also exists, and everything that exists needs a creator." 🐚 Yagnavalkya saw that he had got into difficulty. Because if he said another God created him, the question will remain the same – who created that other God? You can go on answering a thousand times, but the question will remain the same: Who created the first God? And if there was somebody to create him, he cannot be called the first. 🐚 Yagnavalkya got so angry that he pulled out his sword and said, "Woman, if you don't stop, your head will fall on the ground!" 🐚 But Gargi said, "Put your sword back into the sheath. Swords cannot be arguments." And she told the emperor, "Tell this fellow that those one thousand cows should be returned." 🐚 It was so insulting to Yagnavalkya that he never again participated in any discussion. And Gargi took those one thousand cows back from Yagnavalkya. 🐚 She was the first known enlightened woman. [50]

India is a female country and has remained a female country. The whole psyche of India is female, completely opposite to countries like Germany or America – they are male countries. The very soul of India is female. This is why India has never been able to be aggressive. In the whole of history, India has never been aggressive. Violence has never been the way in India. The whole story of India is a story of nonviolence. Looking at India's history, a very surprising fact comes into light: no other country in the world is feminine in the same sense as India. And this has also proved to be a misfortune for India.

The whole world is of a male quality – the whole world is aggressive, the whole world is violent. India alone is not violent, not aggressive. India's history of the past three thousand years has been a history of suffering, trouble, difficulties. But this very fact can also be a blessing in the future, because the countries that have developed under the influence of the male qualities have come closer to the moment of their own destruction.

The mind of man is an aggressive mind, the mind of man is a violent mind. The countries in the West which have developed according to that mind have all been slowly passing through wars – and they are coming close to the last war, the total war. Now there seems to be no alternative but for them to fight and be destroyed.

The only other possibility is that now the wheel of history should turn, the story of the male civilization close and a new chapter begin. This will be the chapter of a civilization of the female mind. [51]

In the East you welcome each other with folded hands. In the West you shake hands. Do you see the difference? When you greet someone with folded hands you are saying, "I bow down to the divineness in you." When you are shaking hands there is no question of divineness. In fact, shaking hands was developed to be sure that you are not holding some weapon in your right hand, to be certain that you are not an enemy. You offer the right hand, you show that your right hand is empty – "I am not your enemy." At the most, that

is what it says. And it keeps you on the same status; you both shake hands. But it has no mystery in it; it is just a strategy, a diplomacy.

The right hand is dangerous, it can hold a weapon; and if you don't see it clearly open, hold it, feel it, then there is suspicion: the man can deceive you. This shaking of hands developed in the West out of distrust. Now the Western historians are agreed about it, about the origin of shaking hands.

But bowing down to each other with folded hands takes you to a totally different level. It has a different context: it makes you feel respected, honored — and not in an ordinary way, but in the most extraordinary fashion. It reminds you of your divinity, of your godliness. Those folded hands are not for you or for your ego. They are for something hidden behind you, beyond your ego — your essential nature, your very soul. Secondly, the folded hands also signify that I am bowing down to you not half-heartedly, that both sides of me are together as a totality — not as a split personality, not holding anything back. Because when you shake hands,

it is only with one hand. It is only representative of one side, half of you. What about the other half? The other half may not be in agreement with the hand that you have given in friendship. It is a split, divided, half-hearted reception — and you can feel it.

When you shake hands with someone you can feel whether the hand is cold or warm, whether the hand is alive or just like a dead branch of a tree. If it is half, it cannot be warm; if it is half, it cannot be alive. It can be only formal, just etiquette — it has no depth. Only once in a while will you find some hand with warmth. And then it generally happens that whenever the hand is full of warmth, the other hand will also come to catch hold of your hand; both your hands will be together. Both the hands folded.... In the same way that the East worships the ultimate, the absolute — with no difference at all, with the same folded hands, it receives the human. [52]

India has never tried to conquer nature. In fact, India has never tried to conquer anybody. The very idea of conquest could not penetrate deeply into the Indian mind. Even if somebody made some small efforts to conquer anyone, the very soul of India could not support this person. [53]

The power that is the consequence of discipline is impure. This is the reason why whenever we want to use this impure power, we have to impose discipline – either by the police or a court of law or an army. Whenever we want to suppress trouble, we have to bring in an even bigger trouble. This is called "impure power," and it is created through discipline.

That Hitler could create so much trouble for this world was due to the capacity of the German people to be disciplined. In India, no Hitler could ever rise to power. One can try thousands of ways, but you cannot create such trouble in India because it is impossible to make Indians disciplined! The power of the German society lies in its ability to be disciplined. This is why Germany will always be a source of danger; it can always create trouble. If there is someone there who can lead the Germans, they will respond as one disciplined society. Discipline has sunk deep into the blood and bones of the German society.

In the blood and bones of Indians, there is no discipline. There is a reason for it. It is fortunate: because of this, however much we may have suffered, we have not made others suffer. We have endured slavery but we have not enslaved anyone else. To enslave others requires much discipline. We could never accomplish such a thing. Why was discipline not practiced in this country? The reason is that the true genius of this country, the spiritual masters, were free of all discipline. And it is the geniuses that the people will follow. Hitler is not a model for Indians, nor is Napoleon or Genghis Khan or Tamerlane. If we recall India's own history, we have not produced even one person to match Genghis Khan, Tamerlane, Hitler, Mussolini, Stalin, or Mao. In a five-thousand-year history, such a big society has not been able to produce even one Genghis Khan. We could not do that. To create such a pinnacle, a base of discipline, a brick-by-brick solid foundation is necessary.

But we have been able to produce a Buddha, a Mahavira and a Patanjali. These are a very different type of people: they do not create discipline. Such persons are free of discipline, and they are very unpredictable. No one can predict what they will do or say or what will happen to them. India has done a totally different experiment in the world — and it is this experiment that may one day be helpful to the whole world. [54]

India has never invaded any country, has never been aggressive, violent, has had no desire to become bigger and bigger, huge; India has never been imperialistic. It has been invaded by many people, and for two thousand years it has been a slave country under Hunas, Turks, Moguls, British people, Portuguese people, French — you just say the name, and India has been invaded by everybody.

And why did such a vast country, almost a continent, yield so easily? They were not interested in fighting. Small groups of people.... What is England? — not bigger than a district in India. What is its population? If all the Indians had pissed simultaneously, England would have drowned, no atom bombs would be needed....

India is a huge and vast country. Eight hundred million people.... You guess how many! They can reach the moon without any trouble, just standing upon each other. And small groups of Turks and Moguls defeated them....

This is not history actually, India has never been defeated by anybody. India simply allowed anybody to invade; they welcomed them. The country was peaceful: there was enough food, enough space — what did it matter if a few more people were absorbed? There was so much to be shared. These peaceful people, without any desire to be aggressive, remained slaves for two thousand years, for the simple reason that they were not interested in fighting. [55]

The world has come to a point...and it has been brought to this point by the Western attitude of action, and always action, and condemnation of inaction. Now the East can be of immense help. Action is good, it is needful, but it is not all. ❧ Action can give you only the mundane things of life. If you want the higher values of life, then they are beyond the reach of your doing. You will have to learn to be silent and open, available, in a prayerful mood, trusting that existence will give it to you when you are ripe, that whenever your silence is complete, it will be filled with blessings. ❧ Flowers are going to shower on you. ❧ You just have to be absolutely a non-doer, a nobody, a nothingness. ❧ The great values of life — love, truth, compassion, gratitude, prayer, God, everything — happen only in nothingness, in the heart which is absolutely silent and receptive. But the West is too rooted in action. And there seems to be perhaps not enough time left for it to learn non-doing. ❧ You will be surprised to know that India never invaded any country — and India was invaded by almost all the countries of the world. Whoever wanted to invade India, that was the easiest thing. It was not that there were no courageous people, that they were not warriors, but simply the idea of invading somebody else's territory was so ugly. ❧ It is a surprising fact that one Mohammedan conqueror, Mohammed Gauri, invaded India eighteen times, and he was thrown back by a great warrior king, Prithviraj. Mohammed Gauri was driven back, but Prithviraj never entered his territory. ❧ Prithviraj was told again and again,

"This is going too far. That man will gather armies again in a few years, and again he will invade the country. It is better to finish him once and for all. And you have been victorious so many times — you could have gone a little further. He has just a small country by the side of India; you could have taken his country and... finished! Otherwise, he is a constant worry." ֍ But Prithviraj said, "That would be against the dignity of my country. We have never invaded anybody. It is enough that we force him to go back. And he is such a shameless fellow that even after being defeated dozens of times, he again comes!" ֍ The eighteenth time when Mohammed Gauri was defeated, all his armies were killed, and he was hiding in a cave and thinking, "What to do now?" And there he saw a spider making its net. Sitting there, he had nothing else to do, so he watched the spider. It fell again and again. It fell exactly eighteen times, but the nineteenth time it succeeded in making a net, and that gave the idea to Mohammed Gauri: "At least one time more I should make the effort. If this spider was not discouraged after eighteen failures, why should I be?" He again gathered his army, and the nineteenth time he conquered Prithviraj. ֍ Prithviraj had become old, and having fought his whole life, his armies were tattered, ruined. He was taken prisoner, handcuffed, chained — which was absolutely against the Eastern way of life. ֍ When another king, Poras, was defeated by Alexander the Great, and was brought before him, chained, Alexander asked him, "How should you be treated?" ֍ Poras said, "Is that a question to be asked? An emperor should be treated like an emperor." ֍ There was a great silence for a moment in the court of Alexander. It was very appropriate for Poras to say this, because his defeat was not really a defeat; his defeat was through the utter cunningness of Alexander. Alexander had sent his wife to meet Poras — he was waiting on the other side of the river. It was the time when, in India, sisters would tie a small thread around the wrist of their brothers — and it was called *rakshabandhan*, a bondage, a promise that "You will defend me." ֍ When Alexander's wife came she was received just like a queen should be received. Poras himself came to receive her, and asked, "Why have you come?

You could have informed me – I could have come to your camp." ✿ That was part of the Eastern tradition: by the time sun was down, people would go into each other's camp – the enemy's camp – just to discuss how the day went, who died, what happened. It was almost like a football game – nobody took it that seriously. ✿ But the woman said, "I have come because I don't have a brother. And I heard about this tradition here, so I want to make you my brother." ✿ And Poras said, "It is a coincidence; I don't have a sister." ✿ So she tied the thread and took the promise of Poras that "Whatever happens in the war, remember, Alexander is my husband; he is your brother-in-law, and you should not want me to be a widow. Just remember that." ✿ There came a moment when Alexander's horse died as Poras attacked the horse with his spear, and Alexander fell on the ground. Poras jumped down with his spear, and the spear was just going to pierce Alexander's chest when Poras saw his own wrist with the thread. He stopped. ✿ Alexander said, "Why have you stopped? This is the opportunity – you can kill me." ✿ Poras said, "I have given a

promise. I can give my kingdom, but I cannot break my promise. Your wife is my sister, and she has reminded me that I would not like her to be a widow." And he turned back. ✿ Even this kind of man was treated by Alexander as if he were a murderer. And Alexander asked Poras, "How should you be treated?" ✿ "You should treat me just as an emperor treats another emperor. Have you forgotten that just a second more, and you would not have been alive? It is because of your wife – the whole credit goes to her." But it was a conspiracy. ✿ The East cannot think of such things. Mohammed Gauri imprisoned Prithviraj – and Prithviraj was the greatest archer of those times. The first thing Mohammed Gauri did: he took both of Prithviraj's eyes out. ✿ Prithviraj's friend was also captured with him – he was a poet. Prithviraj told him, "You come with me to the court. Nobody understands our language, and I don't need eyes to hit my target – you just describe how far he is." ✿ Mohammed Gauri was so afraid of Prithviraj that he was not sitting on his usual throne, he was sitting on the balcony; the whole court was on the ground floor. And Chandrabardai, the poet,

described exactly how many feet high, how many feet away Mohammed Gauri was sitting.... He sang it in a song, and blind Prithviraj killed Mohammed Gauri just through that description. His arrow reached exactly to his heart. ❧ But Chandrabardai was very much puzzled, because in Prithviraj's blind eyes there were tears. Prithviraj said, "It is not right of me, but he has forced me to do something which goes against our whole tradition." ❧ The East has a totally different approach towards things. If the West learns something about the East, the most important thing will be that all that is great comes out of non-doing, non-aggressiveness — because every act is potentially aggressive. Only when you are in a state of non-doing are you non-aggressive. You are receptive, and in that receptivity, the whole existence pours all its treasures into you. [56]

A *sannyasin* by the name of Dandani existed in the days when Alexander was in India. When he was leaving for India his friends had told Alexander that he should bring back a *sannyasin*, because that rare flower flowered only in India. They said, "We would like to see the phenomenon of *sannyas*, what it is."  When he was going back, just on the boundary of India, he suddenly remembered. He was leaving the last village so he asked his soldiers to go into the village and inquire if there was a *sannyasin* around there somewhere. By accident, Dandani was there in the village, by the riverside, and the people said, "You have come at the right time. A real *sannyasin* is always rare, but he is here now. You can have *darshan*, you can go and visit him." Alexander laughed. He said, "I'm not here to have *darshan*, my soldiers will go and fetch him. I will take him back to the capital of my country." The villagers said, "It won't be so easy." Alexander could not believe it — what difficulty could there be? He had conquered emperors, great kings, so what difficulty could there be with a beggar, a *sannyasin*? His soldiers went to see this Dandani, who was standing naked on the bank of the river. They said, "Alexander the Great invites you to accompany him to his country. All comforts will be provided, you will be a royal guest." The naked *fakir* laughed and said, "You go and tell your master that a man who calls himself "great" cannot be great. And nobody can take me anywhere — a *sannyasin* moves like a cloud, in total freedom. I am not enslaved to anybody." They said,

"Alexander is a dangerous man. If you say no to him, he won't listen, he will simply cut your head off!" ❧ The *sannyasin* said, "You had better bring your master here, maybe he can understand what I am saying." ❧ Alexander had to go, because the soldiers who had come back said, "He is a rare man, luminous, there is something of the unknown around him. He is naked, but you don't feel in his presence that he is naked — later on you remember. He is so powerful that in his presence you simply forget the whole world. He is magnetic, and a great silence surrounds him and the whole area feels as if it is delighting in the man. He is worth seeing, but he says that nobody can take him anywhere, that he is nobody's slave." ❧ Alexander came to see him with a naked sword in his hand. The *sannyasin* laughed and said, "Put down your sword, it is useless here. You can cut only my body, and that I left long ago. So put your sword back, don't be childish." ❧ And it is said that that was the first time that Alexander followed somebody else's

order; just because of the very presence of the man he couldn't remember who he was. He put his sword back in the sheath and said, "I have never come across such a beautiful man." ❧ When he was back home he said, "It is difficult to kill a man who is ready to die, it is meaningless to kill him. You can kill a person who fights, then there is some meaning in it, but you can't kill a man who is ready and who is saying: 'This is my head, you can cut it off.'" ❧ Alexander had to report to his friends, "I came across a man who was really something rare — and you have heard rightly, this flower is rare — but nobody can force him, because he is not afraid of death." ❧ When a person is not afraid of death how can you force him to do anything? It is your fear that makes you a slave — it is your fear. In fact, it is your fear that forces you to make others slaves before they can try to make a slave out of you. A man who is fearless is neither afraid of anybody nor makes anybody afraid of him. Fear totally disappears. 57

songs in silence
sutras in stone

In the East
a statue is
made not for its
own sake:
it is made as
a code language
for the centuries
that follow.

A mystic also creates. Buddha creates by speaking; he sculpts in words. He creates in parables, stories, weaves stories within stories, brings insight into the world, but this is not a kind of possession. He is perfectly at ease. He can be silent if he decides so, he will not go mad. And he knows exactly what he is doing; that's why it is called objective art. He knows what he is doing, he knows what it will do to people. He knows if this particular thing is meditated upon, this will be the consequence of it. It is utterly scientific.

If you meditate on a Buddha statue you will suddenly feel yourself becoming cool, silent, tranquil. You will suddenly feel a kind of balancing happening, just by meditating on the Buddha statue. Or, if you meditate on the Taj Mahal on a full-moon night — it is a Sufi work of art, it was created by Sufis; it is a message of love — if you go on a full-moon night and simply sit there, not thinking about the Taj Mahal, not saying stupid things like "How beautiful!"

just meditating, absorbing, you will feel a great insight happening to you. As the moon starts rising, something will start rising in you too. As the noises of the city disappear, your noisy mind will start disappearing. You can have a great meditative experience through the Taj Mahal.

And it will not be only meditative — that is the difference between the Taj Mahal and Ajanta. When meditation happens you will feel overflowing with love. In Ajanta, love will not happen, only meditation will happen. Ajanta was created by Buddhist mystics who believe in awareness and in nothing else. Sufis believe in love; meditation is part of it.

Objective art means it has been created deliberately by one who knows what he is doing, who brings something from the other dimension into this world, some form. Just watching that form, a form will arise in you, a song. Just singing that song, you will become something else, a mantra. [58]

The ancientmost tradition of music is that it was born out of meditation. The people who meditated could not find any way to impart their experiences. They invented different instruments so that something can be said without creating a meaning in you but certainly a joy, a dance. ✿ It must have been a tremendously valuable revelation for those who in the beginning discovered a language which is not a language. Sounds in themselves have no meaning. Meaning is man's imposition on sounds. Sounds are natural. The wind blowing through the pine trees has a sound and a music of its own. Or a river, descending from the mountain through the rock, has its own sound and its own music. ✿ It is my assumption that meditators, listening to the inner silence, must have felt the tremendous difficulty of how to share it. It was in those beginning days that music was discovered. The discovery is simple: take away the meaning from the sounds and, instead of meaning, give the sounds harmony, a rhythm which penetrates to the very heart. It says nothing, but it says the unsayable too. ✿ The ordinary idea of music is that it consists of sounds, but that is only half the truth, and of lesser importance. As the music becomes deeper and deeper, it consists of silences between two sounds. ✿ An ancient proverb in China is, "When the musician becomes perfect he throws away his instruments," because instruments can only create sound. The silence is created by the musician. But at the perfection, the same sounds that were creating small pieces of silence start becoming a disturbance. A strange idea, but perfectly meaningful, significant. It applies to every art. When the archer becomes perfect he throws away his bow and his arrows; just his eyes are enough to look at a flying bird and the bird will fall down. The bow and arrows were only a preparation. ❧ The same applies to music, to painting, to all the arts which man has discovered. At the ultimate peak, you don't need the steps, the ladder which has helped you to reach the peak. It becomes irrelevant. The classical music was devoted to silence and to meditation. ❧ A beautiful story is told about a *nabob* of Lucknow. Lucknow remained for centuries the most cultured, sophisticated city in this country. Arts were respected, wisdom was highly prized. ❧ The *nabob*, the King of Lucknow, was certainly a man of tremendous courage, insight. But these are the people who become misunderstood by the common man. Before I tell you the story about the musician, it will be good to know about the king who invited him to Lucknow, to his court. ❧ He was the last King of Lucknow, and when the British armies invaded Lucknow he was listening to music. He

was informed that the British armies were coming closer and closer. He said, "Just welcome them. They are our guests." Perhaps nowhere else in history has there been a king who accepted his enemies as guests. And he told his people, "Make every arrangement for their comfort, and tomorrow I will receive them in the court. If they want to remain here, they can remain. If they want the power, they can have it. There is no need for unnecessary violence. Things can be settled in a more cultured way. But as far as this moment is concerned, I will not disturb the musicians just because a few stupid people are attacking the city." ❧ This *nabob* was very much concerned that all the great musicians had played in his court except one. He inquired: "What are the reasons?" ❧ His people said, "His conditions are absolutely insane. He says that while he is playing his music, nobody should move. If anybody starts moving or swaying with the music, his head has to be immediately removed from his body. He will come only if this condition is fulfilled." ❧ The *nabob* said, "You should have told me before! Invite him and tell him the condition is accepted. And declare to the whole beautiful city of Lucknow that those who want to hear the musician should know the condition, otherwise they should not come." ♪ But almost ten thousand people came to listen to the musician. And the *nabob* was not a man to go against his word: one thousand soldiers with naked swords were surrounding the listeners. The order was that they should note down whoever moved, because to remove his head in the middle would be a disturbance. ♪ Only twelve heads moved. They were noted. In the middle of the night, the musician asked, "Has my condition been fulfilled?" ♪ The king said, "Yes, these are the twelve people who moved and swayed and forgot the condition. Now it is up to you: what do you want? Should we behead them?" ♪ To everyone's surprise, the musician said, "These are the only people worthy to listen to me! Now let the whole crowd go. They were not listening to me, they were simply protecting themselves. Just an accidental movement could cause death, just a change of position could be dangerous. They were too concerned with their lives. Music is not for them; let them go. Now the real music I can

play for you in what remains of the night — and for these twelve people." It took a strange turn.... ♪ The *nabob* said, "But this is a strange way to find the right people." ♪ The musician said, "That is the only way to find the right people. These are the people for whom music means something more than life itself." ♪ And in fact they had simply forgotten all about the conditions. Music touched their hearts and they started swaying, a kind of dance entered into their beings. He played his music for those twelve people the rest of the night. And he told the nabob that he did not need any reward. This was enough reward, to find the right people who could listen to music. "I would pray to you to reward these people, because these are the people to whom music is meditation...." ♪ There are two possibilities, looking at this story: either meditators found music, or musicians found meditation. But they are so immensely and deeply connected with each other. My own experience is that because meditation is a far higher, far deeper experience, music must have been found by the meditators — as a language to bring something from their inner dance, inner silence, to people they loved. ❧ The ancient music in the East needs not only the training for the musician, it needs immense training for the listener. Everybody cannot understand the ancient classical music. You have to be capable of falling in tune with the harmony. In a certain way you have to disappear and let only the music remain. ❧ It has been the experience of all great musicians, dancers, painters, sculptors, that while they are deepest in their creativity, they are no more. Their very creativity gives them the taste of disappearing into the universal; that becomes their first acquaintance with meditation. So both are possibilities: either music has led people to the point of meditation, or meditation has tried to find a means to express the inexpressible. But in any case, music is the highest creation that man is capable of. 59

The mystic Nanak was always accompanied by a musician, his disciple Mardana. Before he would speak, he would tell Mardana to play on his *veena* and create the atmosphere for him to speak. And as he would stop speaking, he would again ask Mardana to create music as beautiful as possible, "So that these people who have come to listen to me understand perfectly well that words are impotent. The beginning is music and the end is music. I have to use words because you are not aware that there are higher ways of communicating." Mardana followed Nanak...and Nanak is a mystic who stands aloof in a way, because he traveled the most. He traveled all over India, he went to Ceylon. And finally, he traveled to Afghanistan, to Saudi Arabia, and reached the holy place of the Mohammedans, Kaaba. It was evening time when he arrived. His fame, his name, had already reached ahead of him. But the people, the priests of Kaaba could not believe that a mystic of the quality of Nanak, as they have heard about him, should behave in this way. The night was falling and he prepared his bed and told Mardana to make arrangements for sleeping. And they both kept their feet pointing towards the Kaaba! That was absolutely insulting to the Mohammedans.... Certainly, they were offended. And they told Nanak, "You are not a mystic and you don't even know how to behave in a gentlemanly way. You are insulting us." Nanak said, "Don't be annoyed with me. I have my own troubles. My trouble is, wherever I keep my feet, they are always pointing towards the divine. Because except the divine, nothing else exists. I have not knowingly done it, but if you feel offended, you can move my legs in any direction you want." And the story is so tremendously beautiful: as Nanak's legs were moved in all directions, the priest became puzzled — the Kaaba started moving in the same direction where Nanak's feet were moved! Perhaps this is a parable. Kaaba is only a stone, and stones are not supposed to be so sensitive. But one thing it indicates clearly — that the whole existence is full, throbbing with only one music, one dance, one godliness. [60]

Everything that is of authentic value in life has arisen out of meditation; there is no other way. Meditation is the mother of art, music, poetry, dance, sculpture. All that is creative, all that is life-affirmative, is born out of meditation. [61]

There is a famous story about Tansen. He was the musician in the court of Akbar. Akbar was very interested to have the best from all directions in his court — the best musician, the best poet, the best philosopher, and so on and so forth. He had chosen Tansen, and Tansen was perhaps one of the greatest musicians the world has ever produced. ❦ Akbar had given orders that, where Tansen used to live, through-out the whole neighborhood nobody could play music. It would be a disturbance to Tansen. Anybody playing music there would be put into jail, or he had to accept a challenge and come to the court and face Tansen with his music. ❦ So many people came and were defeated; Tansen had certainly something higher to give. But there was a man, Baiju Bawara. His name was Baiju; *bawara* means mad. People thought he was mad, so his full name became Baiju Bawara. His whole ambition was to come to a point where he could defeat Tansen. ❦ He worked hard for twenty-four hours a day. For the final touches he went to Haridas, the same man who was the teacher of Tansen. Haridas was very happy: "I never thought that another man like Tansen would ever be my disciple. But you have the quality. Just one thing is missing: you have a desire to defeat some-body, and that is not very musical. That is making your being unmusical. You have beautiful instruments and you have beautiful art, but your heart is not in the music, it is in defeating somebody. And unless you drop that idea you will never be equal to Tansen. He has no idea to defeat anybody, that's why he goes on winning." ❦ It was very difficult for Baiju Bawara to get rid of the desire, because that was the desire through which he had devoted his whole life to music. But if the master said so, then it was better to wait. He forgot all about Tansen, slowly, slowly. ❦ Once, when Haridas became very old, he became sick; he had a paralysis of the legs, so he could not go from his small cottage to the nearby Krishna temple. And without seeing Krishna, he would not eat anything. Many physicians tried to treat him; they could not do anything. ❦ Baiju Bawara heard about it. He came running from his village, and he played early in the morning, when Haridas used to get up. The music that he played and the song that he sang means: "My eyes are thirsty to see you. Give strength to my legs; otherwise you will be responsible if I cannot see you. Don't leave me." ❦ And he sang with such beauty and played with such greatness that Haridas stood up, went to Krishna's temple where Baiju Bawara was playing on the steps, and worshipped Krishna.

Coming back, he told Baiju Bawara, "Now you can go and have a competition with Tansen. Now you don't have any desire of competition, or winning. And if your music can heal my legs, you have got the master key." ❦ But Baiju Bawara said, "What is the point? I have fallen in love with music, I have forgotten all about Tansen. It was a childish desire. And you were right — I would have been defeated. And you are also right that today I would be victorious. But now there is no desire...." ❦ Haridas said, "Baiju, you are really *bawara*! You are really mad. Now is the point at which you can win." Baiju never went, but because Haridas himself had said, "This is the point at which you can win," it was absolutely certain that he had gone higher than Tansen. And in refusing to go in for a competition, he showed that now his music was not part of the marketplace, it was something sacred. Now it had become his meditation. [62]

In the East we have a deeper understanding of God.... Creation is not something separate from God: it is His play; it is He Himself hiding in many forms. Here He has become a rock, there He has become a flower. Here He is a sinner and there He is a saint. The whole play is His. And He is the only actor and He goes on dividing His roles. He is in Jesus and He is in Judas.

In the East, God is not a person — God is the very stuff the universe is made of. God is not a creator — God is creativity. And the creator and the creation are just two aspects of the same creative energy.

In the West, the idea is something like a painter making a picture, a painting. By the time the painting is complete, the painting is separate from the painter. Then the painter can die, but the painting will remain. In the East, we don't think of God and the world as a painter and a painting — we think of God as a dancer, *nataraj*. You cannot separate the dancer from the dance; if the dancer goes, the dance goes. If the dance stops, then the person is no more a dancer. Dancer and dancing exist together; they cannot exist separately; you cannot separate them.

God is more like a dancer. I am one of His movements; you are also one of His movements — you may recognize it, you may not recognize it. The only difference in the world is that a few people recognize that they are Gods and a few people don't recognize that they are Gods. The difference is not of your being, it is only of recognition. [63]

In Indian classical music this is an ancient, established fact, that you can place a sitar – an Indian musical instrument – in an empty room, in one corner, and on the other side, just facing that sitar, let a master sitarist play. And you will be surprised: if the master is really a maestro, the other sitar sitting there in the corner starts vibrating with the same tune. This is synchronicity. 🎵 An invisible vibe of the music that is being played by the master slowly starts moving in the room. It is just like when you throw a stone in a silent lake, and ripples arise and go on spreading to the farther and farther shores. In the same way, every note of the master is creating a ripple in the air around him, and those ripples are going farther away. While passing the other sitar they will strike its strings. But the master has to be a very refined sitarist, because those strings on the other sitar need a very delicate touch, then they will start slowly vibrating. Great masters have played it, showed it, exhibited it. 🎵 The Moghul Emperor of India, Akbar, was very interested when he heard about this, and he had one of the greatest musicians, Tansen, in his court, so he asked Tansen about it. Tansen said, "I am a great musician, but this is beyond me. My master can do it." 🎵 Akbar said, "Is there somebody who can play better than you?" – because so many musicians had come to try to defeat Tansen. This was a constant thing, to want to become a member of the group Akbar had created called "The Nine Jewels:" nine master minds, one for each dimension of life. Tansen was one of them. 🎵 Tansen said,

"Yes, there is only one man, my master." ❧ Akbar said, "I would like to invite him. We will give him the greatest welcome ever given to anybody, but I would like to listen to him." ❧ Tansen said, "That's why I have never mentioned his name to you. I sing, I play the music, because I am full of desires, expectations. You have given me so much, but the desires are unending: I still go on playing because I want to get something. My master has got it — he plays because he has something that he has to play and spread. I play because I want to get something. I am a beggar, he is a master. He will not come to the court; only beggars like me can come to court. For what will he come? You will have to go to him — the thirsty go to the well — if you are interested. That's why I have never mentioned his name, because mentioning his name will mean you will ask me to call him; and then it will look uncourteous, unmannerly, to refuse you. But I am helpless." ❧ "He is an old beggar in the eyes of the world. He lives just near your palace, not far away, by the side of the Yamuna river. He has a small hut there, you will have to go to him. And you cannot just demand of him, "Play!" When he is playing you can listen in hiding, because seeing us he may stop just to welcome us, to receive us. But every day at three o'clock in the morning he plays, so we have to go and hide outside the hut. And you can take my sitar there, outside the hut, and watch." ❧ Tansen and Akbar both went, took the sitar there, sat outside and waited for the time. Exactly at three o'clock Tansen's master started playing. His name was Haridas. Perhaps India has never produced any other musician of his quality. The moment he started playing, the sitar outside started vibrating with exactly the same tune.... ❧ At three o'clock, early in the morning, Akbar saw with his own eyes the other sitar vibrating, replying, as if the master were playing on both, as if some invisible fingers had reached out to the sitar waiting outside. For the first time Akbar started weeping. Tears came into his eyes, just out of joy. ❧ They went home slowly. They remained silent all the way, but when Akbar was entering his palace and Tansen was taking leave to go to his house, Akbar said, "Tansen, I used to think that nobody could play better than you, but I am sorry to say that you are nowhere near your master. Why are you wasting your time in my court? – you should be with your master. If even a dead musical instrument is receptive to that man's music, what is not possible between you and him? Miracles are possible. Just forget this court, forget me. And he is an old man – you be with him; just sit by his side and let his energy flow in you, let his music make you afire." This is the law of synchronicity. [64]

Western society lives under an affliction — their ignorance about meditation; hence, whatever they do is coming from the mind. And mind is not the source of joy. It can only create agony, but never ecstasy. Mind is your hell.

So learn to be more meditative, and let your creativity be secondary to your meditativeness. Then you will have a totally different state of being — that of ecstasy; and out of ecstasy, whatever is created has also some flavor of it.

In the West, perhaps Gurdjieff is the only man who has divided art into two sections: the objective art and the subjective art. Subjective art is from the mind, and is out of anguish. Objective art — the Taj Mahal, the caves of Ellora and Ajanta, the temples of Khajuraho — has come from meditative people. Out of their love, out of their silence, they wanted to share; it is their contribution to the world. The Western artist has lived under a very heavy burden. It is time that he should be made aware that there is something more beyond the mind. First reach to that beyond, and then you can create stars — and they will not only be a great joy to you, they will also be a great joy for those who see them. [65]

The people who created the Taj Mahal — that is real art — they were Sufi mystics, who knew what meditation is. And they created the Taj Mahal in such a way that if on every full-moon night, exactly at nine o'clock in the evening, you just sit looking at the most beautiful architecture in the whole world, you will find that suddenly you are becoming silent, peaceful, serene. Something is transpiring between you and the Taj Mahal.

Gurdjieff used to call the Taj Mahal, "objective art." It means: created by people who are fully aware, able to create something which can help people to grow....

The people who built the Taj Mahal — it is not a release for them, it is their experience. And they are trying somehow to make something which can also give you the same experience, at least a glimpse of it. In India there are many places of objective art, and it is obvious why they are in India because for ten thousand years the country has been involved with meditative techniques.

The caves of Ajanta and Ellora...there are many caves; the whole mountain has been carved.

Great caves have been made into the mountain, a line of caves — perhaps thirty or thirty-five — and each cave has its own beauty; not just beauty, but its own meditative fragrance from a different angle. [66]

There is a Buddhist prayer hall in the Ajanta caves where the stones used to echo the sound with the same intensity as that of an Indian musical instrument, the tabla. If we strike those stones with the same force as is used in playing the tabla, they will give out the same amount of sound. Ordinary stones used in the construction of domes do not possess the capacity to re-echo certain very subtle sounds, and so those specific types of stones were employed. What is the purpose behind all this? The purpose is that when anyone chants aum, and it is done very intensely, the dome of the temple resounds the same sound back, forming a circle of the chanting or sound. The dome of the temple, by the very nature of its design, helps in the formation of a circle by echoing back the sound. The joy of experiencing such a sound-circle is unique. If the chanting of aum is done under the wide open sky, no sound-circle will be formed, and one will never experience that joy. [67]

On the full-moon night, when the moon comes just in the middle of the sky, the Taj Mahal becomes the greatest object of meditation that man has created. You just sit silently and look at it, and just looking at it your thoughts will subside. The beauty of it is so enormous that your mind simply feels at a loss. It cannot grasp it, so it becomes silent. [68]

In India you will find sculpture a thousandfold greater, millions of temples with tremendously beautiful statues of men, of women — but all devoted basically to meditation. Just looking at the statue of Buddha you will feel some serenity within you — the proportion of the Buddha, the body, the posture, the way he is sitting, the half-closed eyes. You just sit silently, look at the statue, and you will start falling into a silence....

In the East a statue is not made for its own sake: it is made as a code language for the centuries that follow. Scriptures may disappear, languages may change, words may be interpreted. Doctrines can be wrongly interpreted, commented upon. There may be dispute about theories — and there have been — so they thought there must be a different way than language. [69]

How many artists, craftsmen, sculptors, were employed to create one thousand temples, a whole city of temples, how many years it took! — and this is not only one place: there is Ajanta, a group of caves which Buddhists created. The whole mountain...for miles they have carved caves inside the mountain. And inside the caves you will find tremendous works of art, everything is beautiful. Buddha's whole life in stone.

The first cave you enter, you find the birth of Buddha. And those are not small caves.... They have been carved in solid stone. And the whole life of Buddha slowly unfolds in each cave, and in the last cave Buddha is sleeping....

It is the last moment of his life, when he asked his disciples, "If you have to ask any questions, ask me; otherwise I am going into eternal sleep, forever." He has not even a pillow, just his hand is used as a pillow — but such a huge statue, and so beautiful.

There are the Ellora caves, again carved into the mountains. There are Hindu temples in Jagganath Puri, in Konarak. You cannot imagine what art has been doing for centuries. [70]

In Indian temples you will find the statues of Buddha, and in Jaina temples you will find statues of Mahavira and twenty-three other Jaina prophets. You can't make any distinction between those twenty-four *tirthankaras* and Gautam Buddha, except one: Buddha has his hair piled up like a crown, and the Jaina *tirthankaras* don't have hair. Otherwise, you cannot make any distinction, their posture is the same....

And twenty-four *tirthankaras* of the Jainas — even Jainas cannot make any distinction, so they have to invent symbols for each. Underneath the statue there is the symbol line for Mahavira, and other symbols. So if you ask, "Who is this?" they look at the symbol and they can tell you; otherwise there is no difference.

I was visiting a great Jaina temple. The priest was a very learned man, and I asked him, "Can you imagine twenty-four persons over a long stretch of time being exactly the same?" He said, "I have never asked myself the question, and nobody has inquired about it. This is certainly impossible, to have twenty-four persons exactly the same: their eyes, their noses, their faces, their bodies...." I told him, "You should find out."

The next day when I was leaving, he said, "I could not sleep the whole night. I don't see any way to find out; the scriptures say nothing. And your question is absolutely relevant, it cannot be denied." I told him, "You don't be worried because I know the answer. These are not the statues representing personal identities, these are the statues representing the qualities of meditation, silence, beauty, centering. And it was good that the sculptors never bothered about physical differences – they have looked at the spiritual similarities. These statues are not of the physical bodies, the physical bodies cannot be the same for twenty-four persons. They have looked at the spiritual qualities." It is certainly an experience to sit silently in a Jaina temple watching a statue of Mahavira or any other prophet, just looking at it. And you will be surprised that you start feeling certain qualities – tremendous silence, a great beauty. The centering of the statue somehow creates a synchronicity: you start feeling centered, calm and quiet. [71]

The first time I went to Khajuraho I went just because my grandmother was nagging me to go, but since then I have been there hundreds of times. There is no other place in the world that I have been to so many times. The reason is simple: you cannot exhaust the experience. It is inexhaustible. The more you know, the more you want to know. Each detail of the Khajuraho temples is a mystery. It must have taken hundreds of years and thousands of artists to create each temple. And I have never come across anything other than Khajuraho that can be said to be perfect. [72]

A superstition exists all over India that if a statue is a little bit damaged – one ear is missing – it is no longer worshippable; it has to be removed. There are millions of statues so beautiful...somebody's ear is missing, somebody's nose is missing, somebody's hand has been cut – that was enough, and they have been thrown out.

I happened to be in a city near Katni in a small place in Madhya Pradesh. There are thousands of statues – the village consists only of statues – so beautiful that thousands of people must have worked for thousands of years. But nobody lives there. I inquired, tried to find out in old gazettes of the government, and I found only one reference in an old scripture. That village was the

village of sculptors. Being afraid that their statues will be destroyed, they covered their statues
with mud and escaped, burned their houses so
nobody would think that there is a village.

Now it has become a thick forest, wild trees have
grown, but it must have been a very great place
when it was alive. Those statues show that the
village must have contained thousands and
thousands of great artists. Now it is a ghost village. Only statues...they have been discovered
during the British regime; their mud has been
taken away. It was one of the great discoveries.

In Khajuraho, one of the most famous cities of
temples, there were one hundred temples. It
is simply mind-boggling to see a single temple;
it takes almost one day, there are so many statues. You cannot find a single inch which is not
carved...and huge temples. They were also
buried under mud, small mud hills. Only thirty
could be saved; the Mohammedans destroyed
seventy.

They have been discovered again, and there is
no sculpture anywhere in the world — I have
looked into all kinds of sculpture that existed
and exist in the world, but the beauty that
Khajuraho sculpture has is just superhuman —

so perfect that one cannot believe things can
be made so perfect, so beautiful. [73]

But I want to declare emphatically that there is
a vast difference between Eastern art in Ajanta,
Ellora, Puri, Konarak, Khajuraho, and the modern Western erotic pornographic photography,
painting, music. The difference is that all these
temples....
And they have created the most beautiful bodies
in stone. In Khajuraho, stone speaks, sings,
dances; it is not dead. You can see that the artist
has succeeded in transforming the dead stone
into a living form. It looks so alive that any
moment the statue may walk towards you and
say, "Hello." And hundreds of statues....

These statues were not to satisfy your repressed
sexuality. On the contrary, they were used as a
tantric method to release the repressed sexuality just by meditating on these naked statues.
The method was simply to sit there in silence.
Only a dim light reaches there, and hundreds of
statues surround you.

Just watching them, you will be surprised to
find that many of those dreams have occurred
to you — many are such that they have been

condemned in every society. Sexual orgies, but they have happened in your dreams, they are part of your unconscious. And these places like Khajuraho were kinds of universities where people were coming to release, to cathart, repressed sexuality.

And all these statues are on the outside of the temple. Inside the temple there is no erotic sculpture. In fact, inside most of the temples there is nothing — just silence, a cool, peaceful milieu, with the vibes of thousands of years of people meditating there. The rule was when you feel, or your master feels, that now the erotic sculpture outside the temple no longer affects you, it does not create any sexuality in you, any sensuality in you, that it has cleaned your whole repressed sex....

It is the greatest psychological method invented by the East. Nobody is told what is happening, and for years there is no need. Once the master sees, and once you see that you are sitting there and nothing happens, it is as if the walls are empty; when you are absolutely certain that they don't affect you, that is a signal: "Now it is time, you can go inside. Now the door for the inner, for the interior, is open." All that was

rubbish has been dropped — a cleanliness, a weightlessness, and a silence which is full of beauty and song.... Khajuraho or Konarak... these are not pornographic. They are devices for meditation. [74]

Have you gone to Khajuraho or Konarak? There you will see what I am saying to you. Those are Tantra temples, the most sacred temples that still exist on the earth; all other temples are ordinary, bourgeois. Only Khajuraho and Konarak, these two temples, have a different message which is not ordinary, which is extraordinary. Extraordinary because it is true. What is their message?

If you have been to these temples, you will be surprised that on the outer sunlit walls there are all kinds of sexual postures, men and women making love in so many postures — conceivable and inconceivable, possible and impossible. All the walls are full of sex. One is shocked! One starts feeling, "What obscenity!" One wants to condemn, one wants to lower one's eyes, one wants to escape. But that is not because of the temple, but because of the priest and his poison inside you.

Go inside. As you start moving inside the temples, the figures are less and less, and the love starts changing. On the outer walls it is pure sexuality; as you start entering inside, you will find sex is disappearing. Couples are still there, in deep love, looking into each other's eyes, holding hands, embracing each other, but there is no more sexuality. Go still deeper — there are even less figures. There are still couples, but not even holding hands, not even touching. Go still deeper...and the couples have disappeared. Go still deeper....

At the innermost core of the temple — what in the East we call the *garbha*, the womb — there is not a single figure. The crowd is gone, the many is gone. There is not even a window for the outside! No light comes from the outside; it is utter darkness, silence, calm and quiet. And there is not even a figure of a god — it is emptiness, it is nothingness. The innermost core is nothingness and the outermost is a carnival. The innermost core is meditation, *samadhi*, and the outer-most is sexuality. This is the whole life of man depicted.

But remember: if you destroy the outer walls, you will destroy the inner shrine too — because the innermost silence and darkness cannot exist without the outer walls. The center of the cyclone cannot exist without the cyclone. The center cannot exist without the circumference, they are together. Your outermost life is full of sexuality — perfectly good and perfectly beautiful! Khajuraho simply depicts you. It is the human story in stone; it is the human dance in stone — from the lowest to the highest rung, from the many to one, from love to meditation, from the other to one's own emptiness and aloneness. Courageous were the people who created these temples. [75]

There are a few *tirthas*, places of pilgrimage that are eternal — Kashi is one of them. There has never been a time on this earth when Kashi, Varanasi, was not a *tirtha*. It is man's oldest place of pilgrimage, hence it is of great value as a long stream of consciousness. So many people have been liberated, experienced peace and sacredness there, the sins of so many have been washed away there — a long, long continuity — that the suggestion that one can be freed of sin has gone deeper and deeper. To a simple mind this suggestion becomes faith. When so much trust is there, the holy place becomes effective; otherwise it is useless.

Without your cooperation, a *tirtha* cannot help you. And you will be able to give your cooperation only if the holy place has a continuity, a history.

Hindus say that Kashi, the city of Shiva, is not a part of this earth. It is a place apart, separate and indestructible. Many towns will be built and destroyed, but Kashi will remain forever. This is amazing, because so many people have come and gone! Buddha went to Kashi, Jaina *tirthankaras* were born in Kashi, Shankaracharya also went to Kashi, Kabir lived in Kashi. Kashi has seen *tirthankaras*, *avataras* and saints, but they are all no more. Except for Kashi, not one of them remains.

The saintliness of all these people, their spiritual merit, their vibrations, their collective fragrance, have been absorbed by Kashi, and it still exists. This makes Kashi separate from the earth, at least metaphysically. It stands out — it has acquired an eternal form of its own, it has acquired a personality of its own.

Buddha has walked on this city's roads, and Kabir has given religious discourses in its lanes. Now it has all become a story, a dream, but Kashi has assimilated all this within itself and it goes on living. If someone with absolute trust and faith enters this city, he will again see Buddha walking on its roads, he will again see Parshvanatha walking on its roads, he will see Tulsidas and Kabir.... If you approach Kashi sympathetically, then it is not just an ordinary city like Bombay or London: it will take on a unique spiritual form. Its consciousness is ancient and eternal. History may be lost, civilizations may be born and destroyed, may come and go, but Kashi's inner life-flow is continuous.

Walking on its roads, bathing near the banks of its river, the Ganges, and sitting in meditation in Kashi, you also become part of its inner flow. [76]

Yes, I call India not a country, but an inner space. I call India
not something that exists there in geography, on the maps.
I call India that which exists hidden within you, and that
which you have not yet discovered. India is your innermost
space. India is not a nation, it is a state of mind. [77]

Kabir remained a weaver his whole life. Even kings were his disciples, and they used to ask him, "We feel ashamed that you go on weaving in your old age and then you go to sell your clothes in the market. We can provide everything that you want. There is no need."  Kabir said, "That is not the question. I want the future humanity to remember that a weaver can be enlightened, and even with his enlightenment he can continue to weave. The ordinary profession of weaver is not a distraction from enlightenment; on the contrary, his weaving becomes his prayer. "Whatever he does is his expression of gratitude to existence. He is not just a burden on the earth, he is doing whatever he can do. I cannot be a sculptor, I cannot be a great painter, but I can certainly say that nobody can weave the way I weave. I weave with each breath full of prayer and gratitude. And the clothes that I make are made not just to sell but to serve God, to serve existence in the way I can serve it the best." The Hindu word for God is "Ram." And Kabir used to address every customer who came to his shop by the same name, Ram. He would say, "Ram, I have been weaving for you. Take care, this is no ordinary cloth. Each fiber in it is vibrating with my gratitude, my love, my compassion, my prayer. Be respectful to it." [78]

This is the one thing to be understood about Kabir: that he was born as a Mohammedan and brought up by a Hindu. And it never became conclusive to whom he had really belonged. Even at the time when he was dying it was a dispute among his disciples. The Hindus were claiming his body, the Mohammedans were claiming his body, and there is a beautiful parable about it. 🏵 Kabir had left a message about his death. He knew it was going to happen — people are foolish, they will claim the body and there is going to be conflict — so he had left a message: "If there is any conflict, just cover my body with a sheet and wait, and the decision will come." And the story says that the body was covered and the Hindus started praying and the Mohammedans started praying and then the cover was removed, and Kabir had disappeared — only a few flowers were there. Those flowers were divided. 🏵 This parable is beautiful. I call it a parable, I don't say it really happened, but it shows something. A man like Kabir has already disappeared. He is not in his body. He is in his inner flowering. His *sahasrar*, his one-thousand-petaled lotus, has flowered. 🏵 You are in the body only to a certain extent. The body has a certain function to fulfill; the function is that of consciousness flowering. Once the consciousness has flowered, the body is nonexistential. It does not matter whether it exists or not. It is simply irrelevant. 🏵 The parable is beautiful. When they removed the cover there were only a few flowers left. Kabir is a flowering. Only a few flowers were left. And the stupid disciples even

then wouldn't understand. They divided the flowers. ❧ Remember one thing: all ideologies are dangerous. They divide people. You become a Hindu, you become a Mohammedan, you become a Jaina, a Christian: you are divided. All ideologies create conflict. All ideologies are violent. A real man of understanding has no ideology; then he is undivided, then he is one with the whole of humanity. Not only that, he is one with the whole of existence. A real man of understanding is a flowering. ❧ The songs of Kabir are tremendously beautiful. He is a poet; he is not a philosopher. He has not created a system. He is not a theoretician or a theologian. He is not interested in doctrines, in scriptures.

His whole interest is in how to flower and become a god. His whole effort is how to make you more loving, more alert. ❧ It is not a question of learning much. On the contrary, it is a question of unlearning much. In that way he is very rare. Buddha, Mahavira, Krishna, Ram, they are very special people. They were all kings, and they were well-educated, well-cultured. Kabir is a nobody, a man of the masses, very poor, very ordinary, with no education at all, with no culture. And that is his rarity. Why do I call it his rarity? Because to be ordinary in the world is the most extraordinary thing. He was very ordinary — and he remained ordinary. [79]

There was a great mystic in India, Farid. Somebody brought him a pair of golden scissors, very valuable, studded with diamonds. A disciple wanted to present him with something, and they were a rare piece of art. But Farid said, "What will I do with them? If you want to give me something, you can give me a needle and thread, because I am a lover: I join things together." [80]

✺

Farid was a contemporary of Kabir, Nanak and others. I love him. In his songs he calls himself Farida. He always addresses himself, never anybody else. He always starts, "Farida, are you listening? Farida, be awake! Farida, do this, do that!"
In Hindi, when you use the name Farid it is respectable. When you use the name Farida it is not respectable; one only calls the servants in that way. Farid calls himself Farida because he is the master — the body is the servant.

Farid has not written a book, but his songs have been written down by his people. His songs are tremendously beautiful, but you have to listen to them sung by a Punjabi. He lived in the Punjab, and his songs are in Punjabi. It is so penetrating. When you hear Farid's songs sung in Punjabi your heart starts breaking. [81]

anak traveled all over India and outside India — the only great Indian mystic who ever went outside India. And he had only one disciple with him in all these travels. He went to Sri Lanka, he went to Mecca and Medina in Saudi Arabia, far and wide — and he was walking. All that he used to do was just to sit under a tree and his disciple, Mardana, used to play on a certain musical instrument. He would play music, and Nanak would sing a song. And there was such beauty in his song, and in the music of Mardana, that even people who did not understand their language would come there and sit close to them.  After the music was finished, Nanak would sit silently. And the people who had become enchanted with the music, without understanding, because it was not their language...a few would leave, but a few would sit because now his silence had also become a tremendous magnetic force. He was an uneducated man and he used only a villager's language, Punjabi, but he managed to create an impact on almost half of Asia. Without any language, he managed to make disciples. I am reminded of a small but tremendously valuable incident. Near Lahore there was a campus of Sufi mystics, very famous in those days — five hundred years ago. People used to come from far and wide to Lahore for that mystic gathering. Nanak also reached there, and he was just taking a bath outside the campus when the chief Sufi heard that he was there. Neither did he understand Nanak's language, nor did Nanak understand his language; but some way had to be found. ❧ He sent one of his disciples with a beautiful cup full of milk, so full that even one more drop of milk could not be contained in it. And he sent that cup of milk to Nanak. ❧ Mardana could not understand. "What is the matter? What are we supposed to do? Is it a gift, is it a welcome?" ❧ Nanak laughed and he looked around, found a wildflower, and floated it in the milk. The wildflower was so light that it did not disturb the milk, and nothing came out of the cup. And he gave the signal to the man to take it back. ❧ The man said, "This is strange. I could not understand why this milk has been sent, and now it has become even more mysterious: that strange fellow has put a wildflower in it." He asked the chief Sufi, his master, "Don't keep me in ignorance. Please tell me what the secret of all this is. What is going on?" ❧ The chief mystic said, "I had sent that cup full of milk to tell Nanak, 'Go on to somewhere else; this place is so full of mystics, there is no need of any more mysticism. It is too full, just like this cup. We cannot welcome you; it will be unnecessarily crowding the place. You go somewhere else.' But that man has managed to float a flower in it. He is saying, 'I will be just like this flower in your gathering. I will not occupy any space, I will not be a disturbance in your gathering. I will be just a beautiful flower, floating over your gathering.'" ❧ The Sufi mystic came, touched the feet of Nanak and welcomed him — without language; nothing was said. Nanak remained their guest, every day singing his songs, and the Sufis were dancing, enjoying. And the day he left they were crying. Even the chief mystic was crying. They all came to give him a send-off. Not a single word of language was exchanged — they had no possibility of any communication. But a great communication happened. [82]

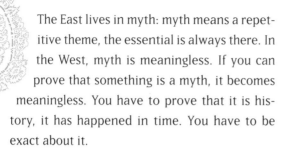

The East lives in myth: myth means a repetitive theme, the essential is always there. In the West, myth is meaningless. If you can prove that something is a myth, it becomes meaningless. You have to prove that it is history, it has happened in time. You have to be exact about it.

This linear concept of non-repetitive life creates anxiety, so when you go into silence, alone, you become worried. One thing is: time is wasted. You are not doing anything, you are just sitting. Why are you wasting your life? And this time cannot be regained, because they go on teaching in the West: "Time is wealth." It is absolutely wrong, because wealth is created by scarcity, and time is not scarce. The whole economics depends on scarcity: if something is scarce, it becomes valuable. Time is not scarce, it is there always. You cannot finish it; it will always be there — so time cannot be economic. It is not scarce; it cannot be wealth.

But we go on teaching, "Time is wealth, don't waste it. Once wasted it never comes again." So if you go into aloneness and then you sit there, you cannot sit there for three years, you cannot sit there for three months, even three days are too much — you have wasted three days. And what are you doing? The second problem arises — because in the West, being is not very valuable, doing is valuable. They ask, "What have you done?" — because the time has to be used in doing something. They say in the West that a vacant mind is the Devil's workshop. And you know it, in the mind you also know it, so when you are sitting alone you become afraid. Wasting time, not doing anything, you go on questioning yourself, "What are you doing here? Just sitting? Wasting?" — as if just being is a wastage! You have to do something to prove that you have utilized your time. This is the difference.

In the old, ancient days, in the East particularly, just to be was enough; there was no need to prove anything else. No one was going to ask, "What have you done?" Your being was enough and accepted. If you were silent, peaceful, blissful, it was okay. That's why in the East we never demanded from *sannyasins* that they should work — no, no need. And we always thought that *sannyasins* — those who had left all working — were better than those who were occupied in work. The East was totally different, a different milieu was there. Being was respected. No one was going to ask, "What have you done?"

Everyone was just asking, "What are you?" Enough! If you were silent, peaceful, loving, if compassion was there, if you had flowered, enough. Then it was society's duty to help and serve you. No one would say you should work, or you should create something, you should be creative. In the East they thought that to be oneself is the highest creativity, and the presence of such a man was valuable. He could go into silence for years. [83]

India is the only country that has not created any opposite entity to God. Christians, Mohammedans, Jews, and Zoroastrians have all created a Devil. Only in India have some people accepted the possibility of a God without a separate Devil. To have to create a separate Devil is not much of an acceptance of God, because then there is constant conflict, and it is never-ending.

I have heard:
Mulla Nasruddin was on his deathbed. The *maulvi* was present to hear his last confession and bear witness to Mulla's final repentance. The priest told Mulla, "Now the time of death is near: repent, ask forgiveness from God and deny Satan." Mulla remained silent.
The *maulvi* asked Mulla, "Have you heard what I have said? In these last moments you should not hesitate" — because Mulla had only a few minutes left to live.
Mulla said, "In my last moments, I do not want to offend anyone. I don't know where I am going, so I prefer to keep quiet. I would rather accept whoever I will have to be with after my death. At this delicate moment, don't insist about this. It is not certain whether I will go to God or the Devil, so it is better not to anger either one. It was a different story in my life, but now in these last moments I think it is wiser to die silently."

If God and Satan exist together then this existence is a duality, and it will be impossible to rise above this duality. So the sage does not say that existence is dual: he says that the world as seen by us is dual, but the existence itself is non-dual. But how to express this non-duality? If we say it is either positive or negative it will create all the difficulties of duality.

There are only two ways of expressing the non-dual: either say both positive and negative, *purna* and *shunya* simultaneously, or say not positive or negative simultaneously. This means that either there is only the void, *shunya*, or that the divine is all-encompassing, *purna*. This will then mean that all is divine....

This has caused a great embarrassment in the West, especially to Christian thinkers. They argue that if everything is God then what about evil, sickness, misery, death? What will happen to all of these? Are these also part of God? But whoever accepts God as all-encompassing will have to accept that evil also is God. The thief too is God — of course, a thief-God, but still God. Christianity has found it difficult to accept this. If a thief is also God, if the Devil is also God, then what is man to choose? Then what will he choose? Then what is evil? In the world of *purna* nothing is evil. If all is God, then nothing can be evil. There are famines, there are floods, there are wars and people die in all these, but it is only the Hindus who have had the courage to say that this too is God. This courage is so vast that it is a little beyond your understanding. Your mind says, "Deny it! Connect goodness with the divine and leave evil out of it." But this sage will then ask, "Then where will you put evil? Then you will have to create a separate Devil."

In fact, if evil is also part of the divine, then ultimately, evil cannot be evil. It can only be a mistake in your perspective because you are not able to see the whole picture. [84]

Meditation is cutting the very roots of problems. I repeat: the mind is
the only problem, and unless you go beyond the mind, you will never
go beyond problems.
It is strange that, even today, the Western psychologists have not even
pondered over the fact that the East has created so many enlightened
people, and none of them have bothered about the analysis of the mind.

Just as in the Western literature – religious, philosophical, theological –
there is no idea of going beyond the mind, in the same way, in the
Eastern philosophical literature there is nowhere any mention that
psychoanalysis or psychology are of any importance.
The West has lived with the mind and the East has lived beyond the
mind, so their problems don't seem to be the same.
In the East that has been the only, single search. The whole genius
of the East has been working for one thing, no other problems: how
to go beyond the mind. [85]

Here in the East, meditation is something that you can float in.
The whole energy around you is just like a river – it is already going
towards the ocean. You don't have to swim, you have just to float.
In the West you have to fight against the current, because for centuries
the extrovert mind has created a totally different kind of energy, not
just different but contrary to the East – the outgoing, the extrovert. [86]

a bolt of
lightning in the
dark night

IN INDIA WHAT WE

CALL EXPERIENCE,

INTUITION, REVEALS

ALL THINGS

SIMULTANEOUSLY,

LIKE A FLASH OF

LIGHTNING.

HENCE, TRUTH IS

SEEN IN ITS TOTALITY,

AS IT IS.

Gulal was the disciple of Bulleshah. This is not something special; Bulleshah had many disciples. There have been hundreds of masters, and they have had thousands of disciples, there is nothing special about it. The unprecedented thing is.... ✤ Gulal was a small landlord and he had a shepherd, Bulaki Ram. But Bulaki Ram was a very ecstatic man. The way he walked was different, his eyes were drunk, his behavior had a certain ecstasy. He was always immersed in joy, although he had nothing to be so full of joy about. ✤ He was a shepherd and earned only two meals a day, but it was enough. Early in the morning he would go to the fields to work, and in the evening he would return, tired. Even then nobody could see his bliss fade away. A certain aura of bliss always surrounded him. ✤ Information about him started to come to Gulal, the landlord. "This shepherd doesn't do much, because we have seen him dancing in the fields.... Yes, he plays the flute wonderfully, but what has the flute to do with grazing the cows? You send him to work in the fields, and we have never seen him working; on the contrary, we have seen him sitting under a tree with his eyes closed. It is true that when you pass by his side, a wave of joy touches you — but what has that to do with working in the fields?" ✤ Many complaints started coming. And Gulal was the landlord; landlords have an ego. He had never paid attention to Bulaki Ram.... So these reports were coming, but Gulal never paid any attention to them. One day, early in the morning, news came: "You have sent him to sow the seeds. But time is passing, and the bulls are still standing by the side with the plough, and Bulaki Ram is swaying under a tree with closed eyes." ❧ Gulal became angry. "This wicked, idle, lazy man," he thought. "People are right!" ❧ He went behind him and kicked him hard. Bulaki Ram fell down. He opened his eyes, and in his eyes there were tears of love and bliss. He said to Gulal, "My master, how can I thank you? How can I show my gratitude? Because when you kicked me there was just one small barrier remaining in my meditation. Your kick removed that small barrier which I had not been able to get rid of. Master, you have done a miracle!" ❧ "My problem is that when I go deep into meditation...I am a poor man and I want to invite saints and sages to a feast but I have no provisions, so whenever I drown in my meditation, mentally I give a feast. In my imagination I invite all the saints and sages. Come everybody! Come from faraway lands! And so many saints had come, master, and what meals I had prepared! I was serving

them and enjoying, so many saints had come and they were all so full of grace — and suddenly you kicked me. Just then, the curd was to be served; but you kicked me. The pot fell from my hand and broke, the curd spilled all over." ❧ "But master, you did a miracle! The pot broke, the mental feast disappeared, saints and sages disappeared: it was all imagination, the net of imagination. Suddenly I woke up; just the witness remained."❧ Tears of love were flowing from his eyes, his body was vibrating with ecstasy. Now Gulal saw this state of Bulaki Ram for the first time. Not only did Bulaki Ram wake up in his witness, he also carried Gulal along in his storm. Curtains were lifted from Gulal's eyes. For the first time he saw that this was not just a shepherd. "I have been searching for a master from door to door and the master was present in my own home! He was grazing my cows, taking care of my fields." He fell at his feet. Bulaki Ram was no more, he became Bulleshah. [87]

The moment the mind is erased — and the method is meditation — you are left with a body which is absolutely beautiful, you are left with a silent brain with no noise. And the moment the brain is freed from the mind, the innocence of the brain becomes aware of a new space which we have called the soul.

Once you have found your soul, you have found your home. You have found your love, you have found your inexhaustible ecstasy, you have found that the whole existence is ready for you to dance, to rejoice, to sing — to live intensely and die blissfully. These things happen on their own accord. [88]

India's way is not of searching with the help of a lamp. India's way is like a bolt of lightning in the dark night. When lightning happens, all becomes visible simultaneously. It is not that a little is seen first, then a little more, then again a little more; no, there is sudden revelation, all is revealed at the same time. The flash of the lightning shows all that is, all the paths that go far away, as far as the horizon, all of them at the same time. There will be no way for the idea of change, because the truth has already been seen.

In Greece, the search for truth through thinking is what they call logic. In India, what we call experience, intuition, reveals all things simultaneously, like a flash of lightning. Hence, truth is seen in its totality, as it is. [89]

Lal is a crazy among crazies. The journey of his life, the Ganges of his mysticism, started in a unique way. Any other information about him is neither available nor needed — where he was born, in which village, which house, who were his parents — all of these things are secondary and meaningless. How his mysticism was born, how his enlightenment was born; how the candle suddenly became a flame in the life of this poor young man from Rajasthan; how the new moon turned one day into a full moon — this is his identity. Nobody would have thought that God was going to enter into Lal's life in such a way. ❧ He was returning home after his marriage with his friends, bands, a procession — it was a moment of celebration. They passed through Likhmadesar village on the way. A unique saint, Kumbhnath, lived there. He was enlightened, ecstatic! He did not care about religion, or sect, or tradition. He was religious but not tethered to any religion. Whatever God had given to him, he shared with both hands. And to him who shares, God goes on giving more and more. This wealth is such that it never ends. ❧ Lal was returning from his wedding, bringing his wife, and this village was on the way, so he decided to go and see Kumbhnath — they could not pass by such a saint whose fragrance had started to reach far and wide. And certainly that fragrance also had flames. It was not the fragrance of flowers, but of flames, of fire! ❧ The fragrance of Kumbhnath was reaching far and wide. Those who could recognize this fragrance were receiving it, and those who could not, who were clinging to their old traditions, were getting disturbed. 🐾 Lal thought, "We should see him; it is good to have the blessings of such a saint." Lal had just married, he was entering a new world — who would not go for the blessings of a saint! But he was not aware of what blessing he would receive. 🐾 When he got there he saw something else. Kumbhnath was preparing to be buried, alive. The ditch was already dug, he just had to enter it. It was the last moment of saying goodbye.... He was distributing *prasad*, sweets, as his blessings. Lal also received some. And before entering into his *samadhi*, his grave, he looked around and shouted, "Is there anyone else to receive?" 🐾 He had distributed *prasad*. Everyone had received it. Now he was talking of some other *prasad*, that which cannot be seen, which cannot be exchanged, which cannot be transferred — but still it jumps and reaches from one heart to another, not passing from hand to hand, but from soul to soul. 🐾 People started looking around. Everybody had received *prasad*, nobody was left. Now what *prasad* was he talking about? 🐾 But Lal approached him and sat in front of him with both his hands spread like a beggar. His eyes were full of tears. Something happened, the same that had happened between Buddha and Mahakashyapa when Buddha had come with a flower. But Buddha had at least given a flower; between Kumbhnath and Lal not even a flower was exchanged. 🐾 But Lal was transformed — he was transformed in that surrendering. For the first time he could see his inner Lal, the inner ruby. For the first time he felt his inner treasure. It was as if in the presence, in the light of this man of truth, darkness disappeared; he recognized himself, he realized himself. He bowed to the master's feet. 🐾 Even in his last moment Kumbhnath had lit a lamp. While going he had asked, "Is there anyone else to receive?" He had found one receiver. Hundreds of people were present, but only one heard the call, only one was ready to surrender — and the one who surrenders is filled. One was ready to dissolve — and the one who dissolves has been born. [90]

It is something to be remembered: all the masters of the world have been telling stories, parables — why? The truth can be simply said, there is no need to give you so many stories. But the night is long, and you have to be kept awake; without stories you are going to fall asleep. ❧ Till the morning comes there is an absolute necessity to keep you engaged, and the stories the masters have been telling are the most intriguing things possible. ❧ The truth cannot be said, but you can be led to the point from where you can see it. Now, the question is how to lead you to the point from where you can see it. ❧ There is a story in Sarmad's life. He was teaching his students, his disciples, and suddenly he said, "Come on out of the class, something is happening." So they all came out. ❧ A man was dragging a bull, but the bull was very powerful. The man was also powerful, but a bull is a bull. So although the man was dragging the bull, the man was being dragged! Sarmad showed his disciples, "Look, this is the situation." ❧ They said, "What do you mean?" ❧ He said, "This is the situation between me and you, but I am not so stupid as this man." ❧ And he said, "Listen! Are you taking the bull for the first time?" ❧ The man said, "I am a new servant, and I come from the city and I don't know what to do — I drag him one foot and he drags me four feet! It has been going on for hours, and I don't think that it is going to end." ❧ Sarmad said, "You drop it! You don't understand the ways of the village, and particularly the language of bulls." ❧ And he took a little grass, green and beautiful, and just walked ahead of the bull, without even touching the bull, and the bull followed him. ❧ And Sarmad started walking faster, and the bull walked faster. ❧ The man said, "This is great! He is not even dragging him, the bull is going on his own." ❧ And Sarmad said, "You take this grass. Don't let him eat; otherwise, you will be in trouble. If he creates trouble, start running — he will run with you, but you will reach home." ❧ And he said to his disciples, "This is what I have been doing with you. All the parables, all the stories are nothing but green grass." [91]

Ashtavakra speaks for truth. He spoke truth just as it is, without any artifice. He is not concerned about his audience. He is not at all concerned whether the listeners will understand or not. Such a pure expression of truth never happened anywhere before, nor has it been possible again. Not much is known about Ashtavakra; he was not a social man, not political, so there is no historical description. Just a few incidents are known, and they are quite amazing, beyond belief. But if you can understand, then a very deep meaning opens. The first incident is from before Ashtavakra was born, an event in the womb. His father was a great scholar, and while Ashtavakra was in his mother's womb, his father recited the Vedas daily and Ashtavakra listened from the womb. One day, suddenly, a voice spoke from the womb, saying, "Stop it! This is all nonsense! There is no wisdom whatsoever in this — mere words, just a heap of words. In scripture, where is knowledge? Knowledge is within oneself. In words, where is truth? Truth is within oneself." Naturally, the father became angry. First, he was a father, and on top of that a scholar. And the son hidden in the womb was saying such things — and he was not even born yet! He blew up in anger, became enraged. The father's ego took a direct hit, and a scholar's ego... he was a great pundit, a great debater, knowledgeable in scriptures. In anger he gave a curse that, when born, the eight segments of the boy's limbs would be bent. Thus his name, Ashtavakra, means eight bends. He was crippled in eight places; eight places topsy-turvy, hunchbacked like a camel. In anger his father deformed his body. ❧ When Ashtavakra was twelve years old, the king, Janak, hosted a huge debating conference. He invited all the pundits of the whole country. He had one thousand cows placed at the palace gate, and had the horns of the cows plated with gold, and diamonds and jewels hung on them. He proclaimed that whoever was victorious would take possession of these cows. ❧ It was a great debate, and Ashtavakra's father took part. As dusk was falling, the message came to Ashtavakra that his father was losing. Having already beaten all the others, he was being defeated by a pundit named Vandin. Hearing this message Ashtavakra went to the palace. ❧ The hall was decorated. The debate was at the point of ultimate conclusion, the deciding moment was drawing near. His father's defeat was already a completely foregone conclusion, a question of now-lost or soon-lost. ❧ Ashtavakra entered the court. The pundits saw him; great scholars had gathered. His body bent, twisted in eight places, he had just to move and laughter came to whoever saw him. His very movement was a laughing matter. ❧ The whole meeting broke into laughter, and Ashtavakra also roared with laughter. Janak asked, "All the others are laughing. I can understand why they laugh, but why did you laugh, child?" ❧ Ashtavakra said, "I am laughing because in this meeting of *chamars*, cobblers, truth is being discussed" — the man must have been rare. "What are all these *chamars* doing here?" ❧ There was silence. *Chamars*?! ❧ The king asked, "What do you mean?" ❧ Ashtavakra replied, "It is a simple, straightforward matter. They see only the skin, they don't see me. It is difficult to find a man more pure and simple than me, and they don't even see this — they see a bent and twisted body. They are *chamars*, they judge by the skin. O king, in the curve of the temple, is the sky ever curved? If the pot is smashed, is the air ever smashed? The sky is unalterable. My body is twisted, bent, but not I. The one who lives within, look at him. You can't find anything more straight and pure." ❧ This was a very startling pronouncement. There must have been complete silence. Janak was astounded, shocked. "Certainly, why are a crowd of *chamars* gathered and sitting together?" He became repentant, he felt guilty — "I too laughed." 🪷 That day the king couldn't manage to say anything, but on the following morning when he went out walking, Ashtavakra appeared on the road. Janak dismounted and fell at his feet. In front of everyone the day before, he hadn't found the courage. The day before he had said, "Why do you laugh, child?" Ashtavakra was a boy of twelve years, and Janak's judgment had been overshadowed by his being a child. Now he didn't notice his age. He got down from his horse and fell at Ashtavakra's feet and prostrated himself. 🪷 He said, "Please visit the palace and resolve my questions. O lord, come to my house. I have understood! I couldn't sleep the whole night. You said it rightly: those who recognize only the body, what depth has their understanding? They are debating about the soul, but attraction and repulsion for the body are still there, hate and liking are still there. They go on looking at death, while discussing the deathless! What good fortune is mine that you came and jolted me. My sleep is broken! Now come!" 🪷 At the palace, Janak had him greatly decorated. He had this twelve-year-old Ashtavakra seated on a golden throne, and asked him questions. 🪷 We don't know anything much more than this about Ashtavakra, and there is no need to know more. It is more than enough. Diamonds are not counted in hundreds, only pebbles and rocks are so common. A single diamond is enough. [92]

Atisha is one of the rare masters, rare in the sense that he himself was taught by three enlightened masters. It has never happened before, and never since. To be a disciple of three enlightened masters is simply unbelievable, because one master is enough. But this story, that he was taught by three masters, has a metaphorical significance. And it is true; it is historical too.

The three masters that Atisha remained with for many years were first, Dharmakirti, a great Buddhist mystic. Dharmakirti taught him no-mind, he taught him emptiness, he taught him how to be thoughtless, he taught him how to drop all content from the mind and be contentless. The second master was Dharmarakshita, another Buddhist mystic. He taught him love and compassion. And the third master was Yogin Maitreya, another Buddhist mystic. He taught him the art of taking the suffering of others and absorbing it into your own heart — love in action.

Because Atisha learned under three enlightened masters, he is called "Atisha the Thrice Great." Nothing more is known about his ordinary life or when and exactly where he was born. He existed somewhere in the eleventh century. He

was born in India, but the moment his love became active he started moving towards Tibet, as if a great magnet were pulling him there. In the Himalayas he attained; then he never came back to India.

He moved towards Tibet. His love showered on Tibet. He transformed the whole quality of Tibetan consciousness. He was a miracle-worker; whatsoever he touched was transformed into gold. He was one of the greatest alchemists the world has ever known. [93]

The Seven Points of Mind Training are the fundamental teachings that Atisha gave to Tibet – a gift from India to Tibet. India has given great gifts to the world. Atisha is one of those great gifts. Just as India gave Bodhidharma to China, India gave Atisha to Tibet. Tibet is infinitely indebted to this man. [94]

Today it is so beautiful that for a moment I was reminded of the tremendous beauty of the sunrise in the Himalayas. There, when the snow is surrounding you and the trees are looking like brides, as if they have flowered white flowers of snow, one does not care a bit about the so-called bigwigs, the prime ministers and the presidents of the world, the kings and queens. In fact, kings and queens are only going to exist in playing cards — that's where they belong. And the presidents and the prime ministers will take the place of the jokers! — they don't deserve anything more.

Those mountain trees with their white flowers of snow...and whenever I saw the snow falling from their leaves I was reminded of a tree from my childhood. That kind of tree is possible only here in India. It is called *madhu malti* — *madhu* means sweet, *malti* means the queen. I have never come across any fragrance that is more beautiful and more penetrating — and you know that I am allergic to perfume, so I immediately know. I am very sensitive to perfume.

Madhu malti is the most beautiful tree one can imagine. God must have created it on the seventh day: relieved of all the worries and hurries of the world, finished with everything, even men and women, he must have created *madhu malti* on his day off, a holiday, a Sunday...just his old habit of creating. It is difficult to get rid of old habits.

Madhu malti flowers with thousands of flowers all at once. Not one flower here and there, no, that is not the way of *madhu malti*, nor is it my way. *Madhu malti* flowers with a richness, with luxury, with affluence, thousands of flowers, so many that you cannot see the leaves. The whole tree becomes covered with white flowers.

Snow-covered trees have always reminded me of *madhu malti*. Of course there is no perfume, and it was good for me that snow has no perfume. It is unfortunate that I cannot hold the flowers of *madhu malti* once again. The perfume is so strong that it spreads for miles, and remember I am not exaggerating. Just one single *madhu malti* tree is enough to fill the whole neighborhood with immense perfume. [95]

∾

You will be surprised to know that the greatest mountains in the world, the Himalayas, are the youngest mountains. In the oldest Hindu book, the Rig Veda, there is no mention of the Himalayas. It is very strange, because it was written so close to the Himalayas. They have mentioned rivers — even one river, the Saraswati, which has disappeared since then — but they have not mentioned the Himalayas. The Himalayas are very new, very young, very fresh, are still growing. Each year they go on growing one foot higher.

The oldest mountain in the world is the Vindhyachal. My village, where I was born, is very close to the Vindhyachal. It is so old, that just like an old man, it cannot stand erect; just like an old man, it has bent down.

A beautiful story has arisen out of its situation. One great enlightened master, Agastya, was going towards the south. And Vindhya bent down to touch the feet of Agastya, and the master said, "Vindhya, remain in this position — because it will be easier for me to pass over you in this position. When you are standing erect — I am old — it will be very difficult for me. And soon I will be returning. My disciples have been inviting me continually, and now, seeing that death is very close, I should fulfill their desire. So I am going to see them, and I will be coming back soon, so don't stand back up in your erect position."

Agastya died in the south, he never came back; and Vindhya is still waiting, bent over, for the master to come back. It must have been thousands of years ago when the master went to the south.... [96]

∾

I love the Himalayas. I wanted to die there. That is the most beautiful place to die — of course to live too, but as far as dying is concerned, that is the ultimate place. It is where Lao Tzu died. In the valleys of the Himalayas Buddha died, Jesus died, Moses died. No other mountains can claim Moses, Jesus, Lao Tzu, Buddha, Bodhidharma, Milarepa, Marpa, Tilopa, Naropa, and thousands of others.

Switzerland is beautiful, but nothing compared to the
Himalayas. It is convenient to be in Switzerland with all its
modern facilities, it is very inconvenient in the Himalayas. It is
still without any technology at all – no roads, no electricity, no
airplanes, no railroads, nothing at all. But then comes the
innocence. One is transported to another time, to another
being, to another space. [97]

The Himalayas have attracted the mystical people for centuries
and centuries. There is some quality of mystic atmosphere in
the height, the eternal snow that has never melted, the silence
that has never been broken, paths that have never been
trodden. There are some similarities between the Himalayan
peaks and the inner consciousness. [98]

And to me, India is a symbol for nothing else except for learning meditation. It is a university of meditation. And it is not just today — for centuries it has been the university of meditation. [99]

It takes thousands of years before the seed of religion goes deep enough and sprouts. And the experiment that was carried out in India was such that it not only sprouted, it flowered too. And you, the people of India, are ready to lose that immense treasure of flowers. And you will lose it, because you don't see anything in it; you have turned your back on it. You no longer see any meaning in it.

And the West will have to start from ABC. If it starts on the journey of religion, the West will have to start from the point where we started five thousand years ago, at the time of the Vedas. And for the West to come to the point we reached it will take another five thousand years. But in the meantime, the survival of man will become impossible.

That is why I say that there is a great responsibility in India's hands, which is that what we have discovered — the clues, the laws, the methods of entering human consciousness that we have developed — even if you want to abandon it, hand it over to someone before doing so. That is the least you must do. But remember that you can only hand over that which has happened within you.

We can present the Gita to the West, but it will soon be rubbish, because the song itself is not in the Gita. There are words in the Gita, but these have already been translated into most of the Western languages. That is not going to solve anything. But how can we give that which was in Krishna? The Gita is only the shadow of that, just an echo; how can we hand over that which had happened within Krishna? That can only be transmitted if Krishna goes on happening within us.

And this is my intention — that a meditator is born within you. If India can give birth to even a few dozen meditators who have the same light as that of Buddha's wisdom, then there is no harm. The question is not whether religion should survive in India or in the West — no, that is not the issue. The question is whether it will *survive*. On which soil the temple will be erected is not the issue — all soil is alike; but you are ruining the temple. [100]

But there is another India: the India of the buddhas, the
eternal India. I am part of it, you are part of it. In fact,
anywhere, wherever meditation is happening, that person
becomes part of that eternal India. That eternal India is not
geographical, it is a spiritual space. [101]

ABOUT THE AUTHOR

Osho's teachings defy categorization, covering everything from the individual quest for meaning to the most urgent social and political issues facing society today. His books are not written but are transcribed from audio and video recordings of extemporaneous talks given in response to questions over a period of 35 years. Osho has been described by the *Sunday Times* in London as one of the "1000 Makers of the 20th Century" and by *Sunday Mid-Day* (India) as one of the ten people — along with Gandhi, Nehru, and Buddha — who have changed the destiny of India.

About his own work Osho has said that he is helping to create the conditions for the birth of a new kind of human being. He has often characterized this new human being as "Zorba the Buddha"— capable both of enjoying the earthy pleasures of a Zorba the Greek and the silent serenity of a Gautama the Buddha. Running like a thread through all aspects of Osho's work is a vision that encompasses both the timeless wisdom of the East and the highest potential of Western science and technology.

He is also known for his revolutionary contribution to the science of inner transformation, with an approach to meditation that acknowledges the accelerated pace of contemporary life. His unique "Active Meditations" are designed to first release the accumulated stresses of body and mind, so that it is easier to experience the thought-free and relaxed state of meditation.

There are two autobiographical works by Osho available in several languages: *Autobiography of a Spiritually Incorrect Mystic*, published by St. Martins Press, 2000 and *Glimpses of a Golden Childhood*, published by The Rebel Publishing House, 1985.

The author's website **www.osho.com** offers a more detailed presentation of his work and meditations in several languages.

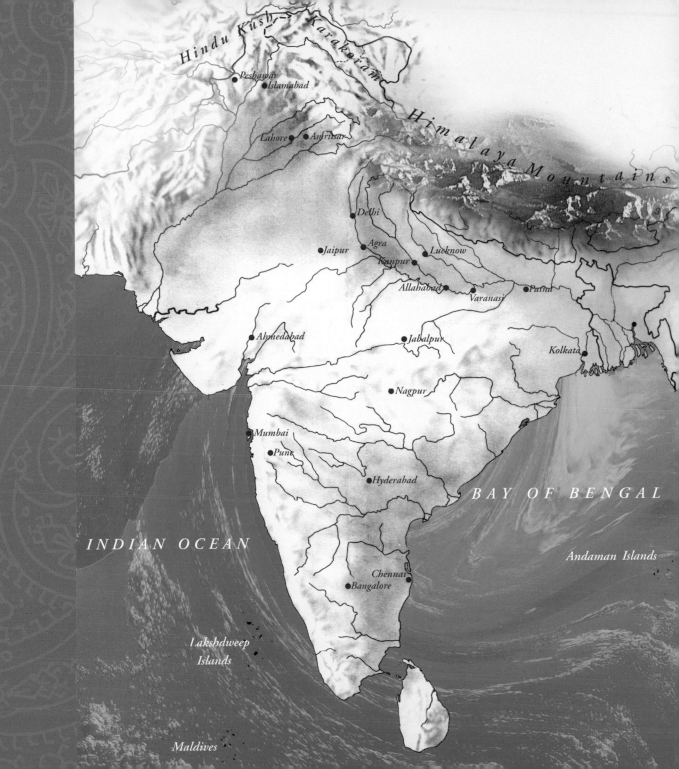

THE RESORT
WWW.OSHO.COM

"The chief attraction is an array of classes on dozens of different types of meditation....

Osho advocates meditation for everyone, but his technique is revolutionary, beginning not with stillness and silence but with intense activity to release pent-up energy and emotions, leading to a state of calmness in which meditation can flourish...an ideal place for people to learn the dozens of meditations he designed...swimming meditation, dancing and martial arts meditation, smoking meditation, walking meditation, breathing meditation and meditation for couples."

The Washington Post

MEDITATION RESORT
at Osho Commune International

A Meditation Resort has been created for people to have a direct experience of a new way of living with more alertness, relaxation, and fun. It is located in Pune, India, about 100 miles southeast of Mumbai (Bombay). Originally a summer retreat, Pune is now a thriving modern city that is home to several universities and high-tech industries.

The resort, spreading over 35 acres in the lush suburban area of Koregaon Park, offers contemporary and traditional meditation programs to thousands of visitors from more than 100 countries. Visitor accommodations range from nearby hotels and private apartments to a five star guest house within the resort.

All of the meditation programs in the resort are designed especially for the contemporary human being. The methods used are tools for self transformation that can become a continuous help in bringing a quality of relaxation, awareness and silence to one's life.

The schedule of meditation activities begins every day at six o'clock in the morning and ends at ten o'clock at night. All programs including individual sessions, group workshops and courses are offered throughout the year, most of these taking place inside modern, air-conditioned facilities. The "Club Med" program — Med as in meditation — is a beautiful outdoor resort facility where one can experiment with a "Zen" approach to sports and recreation.

Outdoor cafes and restaurants within the resort grounds serve both traditional Indian fare and a variety of international dishes made with organically grown vegetables from the resort's own farm. The resort has its own private supply of safe, filtered drinking water. See pictures overleaf.

(Travel and program information can be found at: www.osho.com)

ILLUSTRATIONS

SOURCES

All footnoted quotations in this book have been taken from the published talks of Osho,
a twentieth-century enlightened mystic.

Introduction: The Osho Upanishad, Chapter 21

1   Phir Patton Ki Panjeb Baji, Chapter 1

2   Sat-Chit-Anand, Chapter 12

3   Behind a Thousand Names, Chapter 1

4   Vedanta: Seven Steps to Samadhi, Chapter 4

5   The Secret, Chapter 12

6   The Razor's Edge, Chapter 11

7   Hari Om Tat Sat, Chapter 16

8   Konpalen Phir Phoot Ayin, Chapter 12

9   Books I Have Loved, Chapter 6

10   Death is Divine, Chapter 1

11   The Great Challenge, Chapter 7

12   The Great Challenge, Chapter 7

13   The Tantra Experience, Chapter 1

14   The Dhammapada: The Way of the Buddha, Vol. 8, Chapter 5

15   Om Mani Padme Hum, Chapter 4

16   From Death to Deathlessness, Chapter 17

17   Yaahoo! The Mystic Rose, Chapter 25

18   The Path of the Mystic, Chapter 23

19   Behind a Thousand Names, Chapter 15

20   Behind a Thousand Names, Chapter 15

21   Don't Let Yourself Be Upset by the Sutra, Rather Upset the Sutra Yourself, Chapter 5

22   Mahavir Vani, Vol. 2, Chapter 20

23   Sat-Chit-Anand, Chapter 10

24   Beyond Enlightenment, Chapter 7

25   Sufis: The People of the Path, Vol.1, Chapter 15

26   Bodhidharma: The Greatest Zen Master, Chapter 11

27   From Darkness to Light, Chapter 30

28   The Way Beyond Any Way, Chapter 9

29   The Rebellious Spirit, Chapter 15

30   Beyond Psychology, Chapter 2

31   From Darkness to Light, Chapter 10

32   The Path of Yoga, Chapter 1

33   The Dhammapada: The Way of the Buddha, Vol. 5, Chapter 10

34   Om Mani Padme Hum, Chapter 4

35   Krishna: The Man and His Philosophy, Chapter 13

36   What Is, Is, What Ain't, Ain't, Chapter 5

37   Krishna: The Man and His Philosophy, Chapter 1

38   Nothing To Lose But Your Head, Chapter 2

39   The Path of the Mystic, Chapter 28

40   Come Follow To You, Vol. 4, Chapter 9

41   Come Follow To You, Vol. 4, Chapter 9

42   The Secret, Chapter 12

43   The Divine Melody, Chapter 5

44   Bodhidharma: The Greatest Zen Master, Chapter 12

45   The Golden Future, Chapter 5

46   The Osho Upanishad, Chapter 37

47   The Transmission of the Lamp, Chapter 11

48   Philosophia Perennis, Vol. 1, Chapter 9

49   The Beloved, Vol. 1, Chapter 1

50   The Razor's Edge, Chapter 16

SOURCES

OTHER WORKS BY OSHO

MEDITATION: THE FIRST AND LAST FREEDOM

A practical guide to integrate meditation into all aspects of daily life. Instructions for over 60 meditation techniques, including the revolutionary Osho Active Meditations™.
ISBN 0-312-16927-2   Paperback $12.95

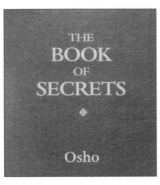

THE BOOK OF SECRETS
The Science of Meditation

Contemporary instructions and guidance for 112 meditation techniques, based on original secret teachings from India. These techniques comprise the whole science of meditation, and there is bound to be at least one method that is perfectly suited to a given individual.
ISBN 0-312-218058-6 1,185 pages $35.00

THE BOOK OF SECRETS (AUDIO)

Keys to Love and Meditation
ISBN 1559274867 $16.95
Two audiocassettes
Renaissance Media

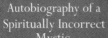

AUTOBIOGRAPHY OF A SPIRITUALLY INCORRECT MYSTIC

A delightful glimpse into the life of one of the most outrageous twentieth-century spiritual leaders . . . answers some of the criticisms leveled at him for his seemingly outrageous behavior and his iconoclastic tendencies. He proves a fascinating man: a prolific writer and lecturer, highly educated, and deeply passionate about his own search for truth. [H]is autobiography is entertaining, insightful and for some, perhaps, even enlightening. — *Booklist*
With 16-page black & white photo insert
ISBN 0-312-28071-8 Paperback $14.95

ST. MARTIN'S PRESS NEW YORK

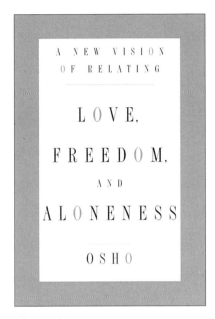

LOVE, FREEDOM, AND ALONENESS

WHY IS IT THAT PEOPLE WHO ARE HAPPY BEING ALONE HAVE THE BEST CHANCE TO HAVE GOOD RELATIONSHIPS WITH OTHERS?

The model of the traditional family is breaking down, children barely into their teens are experimenting with sex, and half of all marriages in developed countries end in divorce.

In this book, Osho explains why these phenomena are happening and how they can actually be viewed as a cause for celebration rather than worry. In a post-ideological world, where all the old moralities are clearly out of date, we have a golden opportunity to redefine and revitalize the very foundations of our lives — to literally start fresh with ourselves, our relationships to others, and how we define fulfillment and success for the individual and for society as a whole. This book is a provocation and a guide for that fresh start.

ISBN 0-312-26227-2 256 pages Hardcover $24.95

ISBN 0-312-20517-1
Paperback $11.95

ISBN 0-312-20519-8
Paperback $11.95

ISBN 0-312-20561-9
Paperback $11.95

ISBN 0-312-27563-3
Paperback $11.95

ISBN 0-312-27567-6
Paperback $11.95

ISBN 0-312-27566-8
Paperback $11.95

OSHO TRANSFORMATION TAROT™

Insights and Parables for Renewal in Everyday Life

Mystics have always used parables and teaching stories to communicate great truths and timeless wisdom. This deck is a treasure chest full of these stories from all the world's great wisdom traditions.

The cards can be used for simple readings to gain new insights into life situations.
Boxed set of 60 cards plus illustrated book
ISBN 0-312-24530-0 $24.95

OSHO ZEN TAROT™

The Transcendental Game of Zen

This deck with its emphasis on the here and now has become a modern classic. Over 150,000 copies sold in North America. In 18 languages worldwide.

An ongoing bestseller for the Tarot shelf.
Boxed set of 79 cards and illustrated book
ISBN 0-312-211733-7 $22.95

AUDIO

OSHO BOOK OF SECRETS
OSHO MEDITATIONS ON ZEN
OSHO MEDITATIONS ON TAO
OSHO MEDITATIONS ON YOGA
OSHO MEDITATIONS ON BUDDHISM
OSHO MEDITATIONS ON SUFISM
OSHO MEDITATIONS ON TANTRA

 **ST. MARTIN'S PRESS** NEW YORK